FIELD GUIDE
TO HAPPINESS

FINDING HAPPINESS IN ITS NATURAL HABITAT

BARBARA ANN KIPFER, PhD

Illustrations by Sandy Hoffman

1/10/08

The Lyons Press is an imprint of The Globe Pequot Press

The Lyons Press is an imprint of The Globe Pequot Press.

10 9 8 7 6 5 4 3 2 1

Printed in the United States of America

Designed by Jane Amara

ISBN: 978-1-59921-184-8

Library of Congress Cataloging-in-Publication Data is available on file.

DEDICATION

To my sixth-grade classmates who laughed at my happy list, thank you. It taught me that my list was special and worth continuing.

Thanks to my editor, Eugene Brissie, for immediately seeing the value in this idea and his great enthusiasm for the project.

And warm thanks to Sandy Hoffman whose illustrations add so much to the book.

Thank you to my husband, Paul Magoulas, and my great boys, Kyle Kipfer and Koir Magoulas, for all the things they give me to be happy about and write about.

CONTENTS

INTRODUCTION

Field Guide to Happiness is a book about using interesting tools to note things that make you happy and about setting yourself on a course to "choose" happiness. It is how to write the "Book of Your Life" in the way most comfortable for you—creating lists, journals, diaries, memory books, and/or mind maps—there are many ways. This is a handbook for taking your happiness into your own hands. *Field Guide to Happiness* is about self-understanding, transforming personal problems, redoing the plot of your life, expanding creativity, and discovering joy through the spontaneity of nonmainstream creative writing.

I know firsthand the beauty of list making and what it can bring to one's life. My list of happy thoughts, started in sixth grade, became the best-selling *14,000 Things to Be Happy About*. It certainly was and is a nontraditional approach to creative writing. The beauty of making the list is the freedom involved; there is no right or wrong way to make my list. I simply spend the time appreciating everything around me and writing it all down.

Interestingly, a large body of work over the last two decades has shown that writing regularly about one's experiences clearly has beneficial effects on well-being and health. It even makes a measurable difference to immune function. It is believed that writing allows us to become more mindful of our thoughts and at the same time create distance from them, replicating in a way the effects of mindfulness therapy or meditation.

Field Guide to Happiness is a chance to walk through the world with a guide that asks you to note the fine points, the wonders. Your brain "takes note" automatically in some cases. When you go for a walk, you do not have to look down at the ground the whole way. You look ahead, and your brain records certain things about the terrain that allow you to walk smoothly over it. But this is not the case for everything. For a lot of the details of life, you have to train yourself to "take note," and this book offers over two hundred exercises for doing so.

Some so-called advances in modern times have actually complicated our lives. We are seeing a movement back toward simplicity, which implies that we are returning to paying more attention to the simple things—the happy details of everyday things and situations. I believe by having your brain always working, it remains healthy. I believe in getting the most out of life and observing how life works and taking notes on it, and the *Field Guide to Happiness* offers ways of doing this. It is inspiration for every reader to stop and take note, in his or her own way, of the little things in life.

PART I : LISTS

This section of the book touches on the use of lists for keeping track of wishes and things one is happy or grateful for—and discusses the importance of the little things in life, the details. Lists can be soothing, funny, a balm to the cluttered, ever-moving mind. Lists make us think and sharpen our minds.

1) List of Things You Were Happy About Yesterday

Uh-oh, you say. You can't even remember what you wore yesterday? So, dig a little deeper and try to come up with a list of ten things you were happy about yesterday. Let's stay away from no-brainers or short entries like "sleep" or "getting paid," and go for some things you felt, experienced, or saw. We are talking things that were more like Aha! moments and details you paid attention to. Were there any moments of pure awareness? Any times when you were in a groove or flow? What favorite thing did you do that you would like to do again?

fresh flowers in the lobby of an office

a rerun of your favorite TV show
    when you're too tired to read

the greeting from your pet
    when you've been
    away all day

making it through the
    green light

getting the last copy of
    the newspaper from
    the store

a bathroom when you
    need it

the luxury of a shower
a worth-the-money meal
smooth travel
standing in front of a fan

Scientists have alerted us to the mirror neurons in our brains that fire up when we see actions performed. We feel, experience, and even understand things happening around us and to other people through the mirror neuron mechanism. This helps us learn by understanding ourselves through the actions of others—a very powerful experience that is essential to human growth. What things did you experience this way? Did you see two people kiss on a TV show and feel happy seeing that?

Make your list poetic, thought-provoking, or reflective of your own personal growth. Challenge yourself to write something that you will enjoy reading again in one year, five years, and even ten years from now.

_____

_____

_____

_____

_____

_____

_____

2) List of Things You Are Happy About in Your Home Environment

It is amazing how much we feel we need to change our home environment. People are constantly talking about or planning to buy new furniture or a new appliance, to paint a room, get different pillows, change to hardwood floors. You've heard it all — or maybe you do this, too. Perhaps this phenomenon is created or fed by TV, magazines, DIY stores — and compounded by the fact that we have little or no control over the office environment, neighborhood, or other places we frequent. So we turn to our homes, feeling they must be continually manipulated.

But how about appreciating your home environment just as it is? Maybe that new dining room set would bring you pleasure for six months, but then it becomes the *old* dining room set. A new material item usually only feels new for about six months. Most of the time, you still have payments to make on a new material item even though it now feels old. Your home environment feels a certain way because your mind tells it to feel that way. Control your mind by telling it to appreciate what you have. Ask yourself, "Will getting something new really make me feel happy?" Make a list of things you are happy about in your home environment *right now*. Consider the conveniences you have that did not exist fifty years ago (or even ten). Consider the comforts you take for granted that your parents or grandparents did not have. Consider what other family members or pets feel comfortable with.

a clear view of seasonally changing nature

your favorite books in the bookcase

the reliability of appliances like the refrigerator

a place to park your car

the comforting sound of a wind chime

a dictionary by the bed

watching a DVD movie in your living room

a blanket spread out on the
     ground to watch the
     stars
answering machines
     and caller ID
the security offered by a
     rubber bath mat
candles lit for dinner-
     time
the art of folding
     paper napkins
garbage-pickup day
knowing where (practically)
     everything is

---

3) Creating a Collection of Resources Containing Lists about Happiness or Things to Be Happy About

Sometimes it is inspirational to read happiness-themed lists created by others. You can open these books or websites to any page and see something you connect with, something that brings a smile to your face. If you keep your own notebook, these resources are great, a springboard for adding to your personal list.

Keeping some happiness-themed books around your home, at your desk, even in the car is a good way to grab some positive language and turn around a feeling of negativity. Read some things to be happy about before bedtime for sweet dreams. Take a mini vacation from a tough workday by noting favorite entries posted on a happiness website. Sit in that traffic jam with a glance at a few lines of positive inspiration. Books about happiness also make great coffee-table books and inspire people to have conversations about being happy. Talking about being happy and happiness with other people is a great way to share and encourage yourself and others to feel happy and experience happiness.

www.thingstobehappyabout.com

www.43things.com

www.listofbests.com

14,000 Things to be Happy About (Workman, 2007)

Choosing Happiness: Keys to a Joyful Life (HarperResource, 2002)

O, The Oprah Magazine

_____

_____

4) List of Things that Make You Happiest in Your Work

Maybe you are one of the lucky ones who has found your calling, discovered your passion, and gotten the opportunity to pursue it. As

U.S. publisher Katharine Graham puts it, "To love what you do and feel that it matters—how could anything be more fun?" It would be easy for you to make a list of things that make you happy about your work. Use your imagination to add some ways it could get even better, especially ways you can initiate. With your initiative, could communications, conditions, and rewards be improved?

On the other hand, for a lot of people, work is seen merely as a means to an end; a way to make money for leisure pursuits, or the way things have to be in order to survive. While not every job or career can be the best or most important one in the world, all honest employment can have meaning and value. Just going through the motions, day after day, is not the way to happiness. Somehow, you need to find a way to transform the forty-plus-hour workweek into part of your happiness, no matter what your job. A first step is to make a list of all the positive factors and bright spots in your work life.

- to love what you do and feel that it matters
- setting aside a whole day to work on a project—a powerful experience
- when your work and words are of benefit to others
- music that induces concentration and seems to have some link (rhythm, cadence, structure) to my work
- using mind-mapping (putting thoughts on a paper map) to think, work, and problem-solve in less time

- working like you don't need the money
- reducing work stress by cultivating calmness and awareness in the work domain
- having pizza delivered to your employees or coworkers when they work late

5) List of Things You Think Will Make You Happy

What distinguishes human beings from other animals is our ability to predict the future, or, rather, our *interest* in predicting the future. We spend a great deal of our working life imagining what it would be like to be this way or that way, to do this or that, to taste or buy or experience some state or feeling or thing. By trying to exert some control over our future, we attempt to be happy.

Write up a list of these things—the "If only I had/was/could do" things. Examine this list carefully. This exercise is long-term. Come back to this list in a day or a month or a year. How good were you at predicting how attaining these goals would impact your happiness? Did you find out that your imagination is not very accurate? Did you really feel the way you thought you would? Or did you replace this list with a whole new set of desires and cravings? It is important to see what this does to us, always wanting more.

- get a major ($) book contract
- figure out my mission in life, at least for now
- see my son get a teaching job
- move to the house and town of my dreams
- have my husband stop snoring
- learn Latin and Greek roots for words
- inherit a lot of money

_____

_____

_____

_____

_____

_____

_____

_____

6) List of Happiness Contributions to Others

Make a list of ways you have contributed to the happiness of others. When you engage in fulfilling the needs of others, your own needs become fulfilled as well. The more concerned you are about the happiness of others, the more you build your own happiness. Any gesture of kindness, gentleness, and honesty affects others, and also how you experience the world.

offering to help with chores
speaking with kindness
giving people their "space" when they need it
really listening when someone tells one of their stories
making a favorite entrée for someone

The way to be happy is to make others happy. Think of ways you can expand on what you have done for others in the past. If you have some money, save or use what you have to benefit others. Feel the joy that comes from deeply connecting with and helping others. We love to read stories about how wealthy people set up scholarships for needy students so that they can attend college. The people who contribute the money must get a tremendously positive feeling upon giving their gift. Not only is their contribution helping an individual, but it is also helping society. Most people cannot make this type of monetary contribution. However, another essential thing you can give is your time. Can you give up yourself to others? Everyone has the ability to give more of their time to help others achieve happiness. From family members, friends, and total strangers, the gift of giving your time is powerful.

- taking care of things so someone can go away on a fun trip
- writing a poem or love letter instead of purchasing a commercial greeting card
- not saying anything about their food choices
- planning a surprise party for someone
- joining in enthusiastically on an activity that someone likes but you usually don't

_____

_____

_____

_____

_____

_____

_____

_____

7) Happiest Moments/Situations List

It is good to take an inventory of happy moments and situations you have already experienced. This serves to remind you to be grateful. It also reminds you that all tough times end, just like good times. Everything changes—this you can count on. This list gives you a chance to be nostalgic and reflect on your life. It also gives you a chance to remember important stories or people in your past, as they define who you are in the present. By thinking about the happy moments and situations in your past, you can gain tremendous insight into the person you are today.

earning my graduate
     degree
a beautiful marriage
     ceremony
giving birth to healthy kids
the first time I skied
a very enjoyable family vacation

Note any patterns to the list you make. Is the list about certain people, things, situations, or time periods? Do you believe you are recalling the items on your list completely and accurately? Look at your list of peak experiences and be grateful for them. Open to the happiness of this list and expand your awareness of the overall themes involved.

---

8) List of People/Things You Think You Cannot Live Without

Do you know someone who has lost everything in a fire or other natural disaster? When that event occurred, they may have been able to save some items—but it's more likely they lost things they felt were dear to them.

Make a list of things, including people, you believe you cannot live without. Try to assemble the list naturally, as the items come to your mind. In the back of your mind, it is important to keep in perspective that things can be replaced and people cannot. You could look at this list in a utilitarian way—a list you could use in a disaster situation. More to the point, the list informs you about what you truly value. What price would you pay now for these things? What kind of fulfillment do these goods or services provide for you? Look

at the list gently, without judging. Can you imagine changing the list, simplifying your needs and desires?

> husband and children
> cats
> handbag with contents
> unpublished manuscripts
> photographs and videos
> children's artwork

---

9) With at Least One Other Person (Especially Someone Close or Important to You), Take the Word *Happiness* **and Make a List of Fifty Words That Come to Mind**

Word association is a revealing activity. With at least one other person, sit down for a set amount of time (five minutes?) and write HAPPINESS at the top of a blank piece of paper. Then write fifty words (or two-word phrases) that come to mind. Do this exercise freely and without judging which words come to you. You will be surprised by how many words "sound happy" to your ears.

absolutely absorbing abundance ace active admirable adore agree alert alive amazing AI appealing approval aroma attraction award awareness bargain beaming beautiful best better boost breakthrough bright brilliant brimming charming clean clear colorful comfy compassion compliment confidence cool courage courteous cuddly dazzling delicious delightful divine dreamy dynamic easy ecstatic energy enhance enjoy enticing excellent exceptional exciting exhilaration expert exquisite eye-catching fab fabled fair famous fantastic fascinating favorite finesse finest flair flattering flourishing free freshness friendly fun galore generous genius gentle giggle glamorous glitter glorious go-ahead goodness gorgeous graceful grand great happiness happy healthy heartwarming heavenly humility ideal immaculate impressive incredible inspire interesting invigorating inviting irresistible joy juicy keen kind kindness kissable learning leisure life light lovely loving-kindness lucky luscious luxurious magic matchless miracle mouthwatering nice nutritious opulent outstanding palatial paradise pamper passionate perfect please pleasure plenty positive precious prestige

priceless prime prize proud pure quality quench
quiet radiant ravishing refined refreshing relaxation reliable rest rewarding rich right rosy safety
save satisfaction select sensitive sensational se-
rene share simplicity skillful smile smooth soft spar-
kling special spectacular splendid spotless star
strong stunning stylish success succulent superb
superlative supreme sweet swell symphony tasty
tempting terrific thrilling thriving treasure treat trust
ultimate ultra unbeatable unblemished unique
unsurpassed valuable valued versatile victor vig-
orous vivacious warm wealth whiz winner wise
wonderful worthy wow young zap zeal zest

The list you've made is a snapshot in time. It is probably the first time in your life that you thought about words in terms of happiness or happy feelings. It can tell you a lot about yourself. By thinking about words in terms of happiness or happy feelings, you will begin to train your mind to think in these terms more often. When things are going badly for you, you can spend a few minutes thinking of happiness words to help you get by. It may be even more revealing to examine the other person's (or other people's) list(s). The people involved in the activity can choose to read each other's lists or decide as a group to offer their own interpretations. When you complete this exercise with other people, you will feel the positive power created by the group effort.

_____

_____

_____

_____

_____

10) Make a List of All Your Routines with Notes about How to Change Each

Most people swear by routines. Many of us feel that routines are absolutely necessary tools for dealing with everyday stress and anxiety. As we age and mature, routines provide a comfort zone—a way for us to navigate the daily demands of life. The dependence on routines, however, can border on obsession, and we often feel that an unexpected change, interruption, or disruption of our routine is upsetting, or even devastating. So, while our routines may often help us, our inability to change them when needed can lead to suffering in our lives.

Make a list of your daily routines. Also make other lists of routines you do weekly, monthly, seasonally, annually. This can include the holidays, which are often stressful due to the requirements we feel obligated to fulfill. Now, choose one of these routines and write out a way you might change it. We don't think much about these routines, often executing them on autopilot. Experiment by changing a routine, trying the new method for a few days. How did this feel? Do you want to continue on to other routines—examining them for

potential changes? Which routines are enjoyable and which are not?
Which routines are healthy, or unhealthy?

cup of coffee
check e-mail and news
exercise
get ready for work
work
make dinner
meditate
read and possibly watch TV
get ready for bed

---

11) Make a List of Things to Forgive Yourself For, Then to Forgive Others For

There are many ways you have betrayed, harmed, or abandoned your-self through words, thoughts, or deeds—both knowingly and unknow-ingly. For each of the ways you have hurt yourself through action or inaction, out of fear or anger or pain or confusion—you now need to extend a full and heartfelt forgiveness. Making a list of the things to forgive yourself for is the first step. Just as you have to love yourself first in order to love others, so do you also need to forgive yourself first.

getting married too young
selling the Chevrolet Camaro
not telling your mother how you felt
    before she died
gaining weight
not taking a job opportunity that would
    have been a better path

Next, make a list of the ways others have hurt you deeply. These are the things you would like to forgive but have not yet been able to. To the extent that you are ready, offer them forgiveness. Understand how letting go of hurt and suffering can bring you happiness, can repair relationships, and even make others happier.

my father's leaving when I was seven years old
the boy in high school who did not ask me to the prom
my mother's way of bringing us up
my husband for leaving me
losing a job through downsizing

When completing this exercise, it is important to remember that just by being a human being on this Earth, you will hurt yourself and other people. The intent is not the point of this exercise. Don't beat yourself up in your mind, and don't sit in judgment. This exercise is about forgiving yourself and others.

---

12) Write Down Your Fears and Worries and Analyze How Valid They Are

Make a list of your fears and worries, ones that come up all the time or recur regularly. Imagine how much energy and time you have focused on these worst-case scenarios. This is time that you can never get back.

worried about son in college
worried about paying for next one to go to college
worried about driveway when it snows
fear of injury so I cannot work
fear of running out of ideas
for new books

Start with the first one and imagine letting go of it; then keep going, releasing each and every fear and worry. Can you learn not to worry about things you cannot control, the things that *might* happen? Can you see how channeling your energy and time in a positive direction will make your life more fun, happy, and fulfilling?

Try giving yourself two minutes each morning to worry about your fears, and then let them go for the rest of the day. Here's a list to help you counteract fear and worry:

- Detach yourself from negative sources—media, people, etc.
- If you feel threatened, leave or seek help.
- Visualize positive outcomes for situations, or look for the positive side to the story; eventually, you won't even focus on this.
- Let go of all worry and fear.

---

13) Draw Up a List of Things You Have Always Wanted to Do (and Go for It)

Wishes can be artistic (write a sonnet), athletic (do a headstand), practical (learn how to repair a faucet), whimsical (be a taster at an ice-cream factory), or fantasy (live in the south of France). These come to mind off and on, but few people write theirs down—and even fewer people do anything about them. Throughout each phase of your life, you can write down your wishes and goals and then review them from time to time. In your review, you can determine why certain wishes or goals were or were not attempted. If a wish or goal was not attempted, then now may be the right time to try it.

Create a "life goals" or wish list of all the things you want to do or learn. The next step is to pick one, and start another list of things you can do to work toward attaining that particular goal. Go for it! This is a great exercise to do with another person or people (a friend, your spouse, your kids) so that you can encourage each other. Sometimes all you need is a little push to achieve a wish or goal.

learn more about cooking
read more about yoga
improve drawing skills
read Thoreau
write a huge commonplace book (see #29)

14) List the Places You Are Fascinated With and Try to Transport Yourself There by Writing about Their Features in Detail

Documentaries, travelogues, movies, and even television can certainly provide us with glimpses of other worlds, locales, and sites so fascinating that we feel transported. But words can also carry us there. You may have experienced this while reading books and magazine articles.

Make a list of places you are fascinated with. Then go to some books, travel guides, or the Internet and describe a scene for each. When you do this, describe the details of a place, as if you were there. This exercise shows how words can take you places and allow you to experience things in a way that makes you feel happy. It is not necessary to actually visit these places. Reading or writing about different locales can offer you all kinds of happy moments.

Stonehenge
Alaska and British Columbia
Nova Scotia
Greece
Machu Picchu

---

15) List of Ways You Can Create Good Karma

Karma means "you don't get away with nothing" (Ruth Dennison)—that everything you think, do, or say has an impact. Karma is cause and effect: What you do today, good or bad, comes back to you tomorrow, and this is your responsibility. The consequence of an action, thought, or word may not be instantly evident, but it will come, and there is no escaping personal accountability for what you consciously think, say, and do.

Understanding this is one thing, but you must constantly remind yourself. You must take the time to consider whether what you are about to do or say, even think, is beneficial or harmful. Your thoughts, words, and deeds create the experience that is your future. You need to become fully conscious of all that you are and all that you can be. It is about how to purify your heart and mind by living an impeccable and enlightened life. You can break patterns of familiarity; you can change the next moment; you can do something different, something enlight-

ened, something creative, imaginative, and fresh; something compassionate and wise. You can transform your own existence as well as the lives of those around you.

Today, make a list of ways you can create good karma. There's a book of 8,879 ways (*Instant Karma*, Workman, 2003), so you should be able to come up with a pretty long list on your own. Look at the present circumstances of your life and list things you can do right now to create good karma. Just imagine how much better the world would be if more people did the same.

- Test your intelligence by challenging it.
- Put a rug down for bare feet.
- Initiate a program of social reform.
- Volunteer at your child's school.
- Give someone a picnic for their airplane trip.

16) List of Meditation Methods that Work for You

Whether you have tried formal meditation or not, you would be surprised to learn how many meditative methods you have already employed at various times of your life. Have you given birth? Childbirth breathing methods are a form of meditation. Ever count to ten before responding to someone? There's another. Meditation is being quiet, finding a center, being in the present moment, seeking awareness and calm. Although it is spiritual, it is not necessarily "religious," and you can use methods of formal meditation as well as techniques for being mindful and "awake" throughout each day. Many scientific studies reveal that meditation is extremely beneficial to people who practice it, both psychologically and physically.

The simplest formal meditation method is watching the breath. Sit comfortably, in whatever position that is for you. Let your eyes close gently. Invite your body to relax and release into the ground or cushion. Become sensitive to and listen to your breath. Breathe through your nose. Feel the air as it goes in and out of the nostrils. Feel the rising and falling of the chest and abdomen. Allow your attention to settle where you feel the breath most clearly. Focus there. Follow the breath. Allow the breath to be as it is without controlling it. Thinking will start. It is a habit. See each thought like a railroad car of a train going by. See it, acknowledge it, let it go, and come back to the breath. It does not matter how many times you get caught up in a thought or for how long. Begin again and bring awareness back to the breath. If a physical sensation or pain arises, do the same. See it, acknowledge it without getting caught up in it, let it go, and come back to the breath. For twenty minutes, follow your breath with close attention. When your mind wanders, stop and come back to the breath.

During your daily activities, you can use breathing to stay in the moment and really be there when you wash the dishes, brush your teeth, assemble a meal—instead of going through life on autopilot. So please take a meditation class or use a book like *Self-Meditation* (Workman, 2006), or have a look online, or come up with your own list of meditations that you would like to try.

Create a "stop-sign" practice out of the experience of toasting bread. Putting the bread in is a reminder to stop, breathe, calm yourself, and experience peace.

When you are in the middle of chaos, be aware that it too will pass—so relax, breathe, and accept the chaos.

Before you go to sleep, make a list of ten things that made you feel happy during the day that just passed. Not big things; the little things.

Do one thing at a time.

During the course of your day, try using the "metta" phrases to send loving-kindness to strangers and associates. Note the difference between feeling isolated and feeling connected by means of your practice.

_____

_____

_____

_____

_____

_____

_____

17) Make a List of How You Can Minimize Suffering and a List of How You Can Maximize Joy

Suffering is a part of all our lives, but the amount we experience in our own lives is optional. You believe in your wants and desires, as well as your aversions and hates. But you see how wanting that coat or that pint of ice cream turns into suffering when you realize that it was an indulgence you could not afford, or it did not bring you more than a brief moment of happiness. How often after this happens do you move on to a new craving or desire? It is a hamster wheel you'd do better to dismount.

The question to continually ask yourself is: "Does this want or desire (or thought, action, deed) create well-being or does it create suffering?" When you are mindful of always wanting things to be different than the way they are, you acknowledge the cause of suffering in your life. It becomes a state of mind. You have to remember that *you* control the state of mind that you are experiencing, and only you can change it from negative to positive.

One way to help alleviate or minimize your own suffering is to alleviate the suffering of others. You have the ability to help yourself through helping others. This creates the perfect win-win situation. Start a list now of ways you can minimize suffering and maximize joy for others— and, by extension, yourself.

- Minimize distortion by turning down the volume of your inner dialogue.
- The more attention you bring to the direct experience of eating, the more interesting it becomes. Eat slowly and savor the moment.
- Awakening compassion and lessening selfishness is more important than any other spiritual practice.
- Centering allows you to live at the maximum, at the peak.
- Praise children often.

_____

_____

_____

_____

_____

_____

_____

18) Make a List of What You Value Most—Your Quality Core Values—and Elaborate on What You Can Do to Strengthen Them in Your Life

Are you living according to your deepest heartfelt values and principles? You can increase happiness by dedicating yourself to goals that really matter to you. The first step is self-examination and making a list of your values, so you can keep track of what is really important to you. Be honest in your evaluation. Don't worry about what other people may think about your list. This list needs to come from the heart.

Let's say that your top five to six quality core values are compassion, creativity, fitness, intelligence/love of learning, and kindness. Here you will see how you can take a list like this and elaborate on what you can do to strengthen these standards in your life.

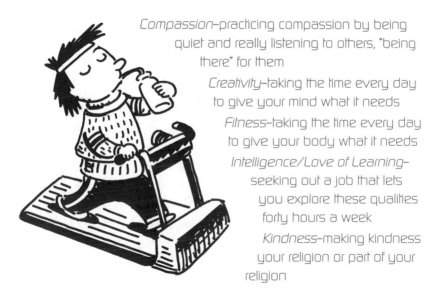

Compassion–practicing compassion by being quiet and really listening to others, "being there" for them

Creativity–taking the time every day to give your mind what it needs

Fitness–taking the time every day to give your body what it needs

Intelligence/Love of Learning–seeking out a job that lets you explore these qualities forty hours a week

Kindness–making kindness your religion or part of your religion

Putting action together with your cherished values produces authentic positive emotion in the doer: pride, joy, fulfillment, harmony, satisfaction. The more you find ways to live your values on a daily basis, the more satisfied you will be with your life. The longer your list becomes, the easier it is to match the action to the word.

_____

_____

_____

_____

_____

_____

19) Make a List of Your Talents and Open Your Mind to the Hidden Abilities That You Have Not Admitted to Having

Each of us has talents (being able to spell well, having perfect pitch) and strengths (integrity, great work ethic, originality). In some cases, talents can be further developed, but in all cases, strengths can be built and added to your repertoire. Developing talents and strengths to reach the next level does take effort.

With patience, persistence, and practice, you can take your strengths to higher levels. Strengths are measurable and acquirable and often produce positive consequences. Very few things are as rewarding as when you can take a talent or strength to the next level.

What are your personal strengths and talents? Can you open your mind to see some hidden abilities that you have not admitted to having? For example, are you truly curious about things? Do you constantly want to know the origins of words or the dynamics of how processes work? How can you then take a strength like curiosity/interest and transform it into an actively engaging novelty as opposed to the passive absorption of information? What strengths and talents are relevant to your job or career?

Make a list of five to ten strengths and ask yourself which of these feel real and authentic to you, which ones you don't question are yours. Now examine each for the level of excitement, yearning, even joy that you feel about them. These feelings indicate your top strengths. Now jot down some notes on how you can use them as frequently as possible.

like to learn
great work ethic
self-motivated, don't procrastinate
exercise body and mind
always have something interesting to do

20) Make a List of All the Lists You Would Like to Create or Have and an Inventory of the Lists You Have Now

Are you a natural-born list maker, or do you envy those who keep and maintain lists to keep their lives running smoothly? If you are the former, what lists do you live by now? What types of lists would you like to start that would be fun or helpful to you? Is your grocery list in electronic form? Do you keep a master list of annual activities and when they need to be on your schedule? Do you check off items on a list after they are completed? Do you look at one of your lists every day, or periodically? Maybe you have hesitated and now this book will motivate you to add some lists to your life. To list makers, lists are a very natural part of our lives.

ten things to do in the dentist's office
best books I have read
ten things to do on a rainy day
major project list
ten things to do while waiting in line

If you are the other type, start slowly. Put Post-it notes or other note-pads in strategic positions: bedside, kitchen, bathroom, desk, car, purse, briefcase, or wallet. Stop and write things down when you think of them—things to do, things to say, things to remember, things to buy. Your choices will be personal.

From there, you might move on to a notebook and keep a list (or lists) for other reasons. Lists of things that make you happy? A grati-tude list? Sample menus? A wish list? A warning to people who are not natural-born list makers: When you begin creating lists, it does become addictive. You may even wonder how you survived without them in the past. It is a very empowering activity because you feel like you have more control of your life.

_____

_____

_____

21) Every Time You Want Something from this Life, Write the Sucker Down

Perhaps you feel regret or you often second-guess your choices. The greatest griefs are those we cause ourselves, Sophocles said. Instead of doing these two things, which clearly bring unhappiness, keep a list of things you want from this life. We're not talking about possessions, but a list of what you would like to have felt, experienced, said, or accomplished in your one lifetime.

Life is complex, and there are often too many choices. By consciously examining what you want and assembling this list, you will have a clearer idea of the choices you have to make along the way. Scholar and political theorist John Schaar once said:

The future is not a result of choices among alternative paths offered by the present, but a place that is created—created first in the mind and will, created next by activity. The future is not some place we are going to, but one we are creating. The paths are not to be found, but made, and the activity of making them changes both the maker and the destination.

We have the ability to create the future the way we want it to be.

visit Block Island in the summer

find the place I want to live for the rest of my life

write a couple of books a year

be asked to speak at a commencement

make enough money off a book to retire whenever I want to

_____

_____

_____

_____

_____

_____

_____

_____

22) Make a List of Books You Have Read That Changed Your Life

Take the time to make a list of books that have changed your life. Explore how reading has helped shape your life, your work, your relationships. Include the books that you feel people simply must read, or their lives will somehow be diminished. Include the books that you felt like you were watching as you read them. Respect the power of reading to shape your life and your world.

To think about this, go back to the books you checked out of the library as a kid. Look on the bookshelves in your house and the books stored at your parents' house to help remind you of the cherished memories. Wander around a bookstore to stir some memories. In most cases, after just a little thought, you will be able to recall many of the books that changed your life.

Did you find books that made you feel that you were not alone in the world? What books made you feel that there was someone else like you, who faced the same fears, the same confusions, the same grief, the same joys? What books took place in time periods or places that you would like to visit? What books challenged your core belief system? What books made you cry or laugh out loud? Reading is a way to live more lives, to experience more worlds, to meet people you care about and want to know more about, and especially to understand others and develop a compassion for what they confront and endure. Celebrate what you have read in your life by making this list.

Little Women

Walden

The Horse and His Boy (The Chronicles of Narnia)

Seeking the Heart of Wisdom: The Path of Insight Meditation

Webster's New World Dictionary

Encyclopaedia Britannica

Joy of Cooking

The Art of the Moment: Simple Ways to Get the Most from Life

Grace Notes: A Book of Daily Meditations

Astonish Yourself! 101 Experiments in the Philosophy of Everyday Life

----

----

23) Create a List of Questions You Would Like Answers to, Things You Wonder About—Truth, Information, Satisfaction

Don't think your questions don't matter. Not only are they important (especially the recurring ones), but their answers may also hold keys to your happiness. Questions have been challenging us since the beginning of humankind. Knowledge acquisition is usually based on questions being answered. Make a list of questions you would like answers to, things you wonder about. Did you have a moment when you first wondered, "Why am I looking out on the world from this body?" Did you find an answer to that question? The answer lies in finding your path, mission, vocation, passion. Maybe all of your questions are not soul-searching or profound, but finding the answers may greatly contribute to your happiness.

The list of questions you write up may be a search for information, for satisfaction, or for truth. The list will tell you about yourself—whether you think philosophically or practically, whether you are a dreamer or a planner. Thinking about the questions you come up with will expand your knowledge about yourself and the world or universe that you live in. Answering difficult questions is always cause for a little celebration. The things you wonder about can become a personal quest for answers. You will find that most answers create more questions.

Can you prove you exist?
Do we each have our own soul mate?

Is a person either
    creative, or not?
How can we be
    happy?
Is love real or
    imagined?

_____ __ _____

_____ _____ _____

___ __ __ _____ ____ __ ___ __ ___ _____

_ __ __ ___ _____ _____ _____ _____

_____ ___ _____ _____ _____

_____ _____

_____ ___ __ ___ _____

_ _____ _____ _ _____

24) Make a List of Things You Have to Do That Make You Feel Anxious, and Assign One or Two per Day So You Can Complete Them by a Deadline

There are many times when each of us feels overwhelmed, anxious about all that has to be done. Maybe it is the holidays or the move from one season to another, or the planning of a major event. You probably can do this exercise right now: Make a list of things you have to do. Then take a calendar or ruled sheet and assign one or two items to each day, so you can complete them by a specific deadline.

finish two big projects by the same deadline
come up with a work plan for the following year
devise a book idea that is really unique

help my child figure out his college major

deal with in-laws on holidays

While such a list, once completed, will give way to another list eventually, there is nonetheless great satisfaction when you chip away at and then finish a list like this. Make sure you cross off the items on your list so you can see the progress you are making, one step at a time. Your anxiety will decrease with every completed task.

_____

_____

_____

_____

_____

_____

_____

25) Make Lists of What Makes You Happy in Your Life Roles: Mom/Dad, Worker/Manager, Student/Teacher, Friend/Lover, Etc.

Write down a list of all the roles you have in life. Cover everything you can think of, from parent to son/daughter to cook/gardener/meditator, and so on. We wear so many hats in our hectic lives that just making a list with all the different roles we play will be enlightening. Once you have finished your list, expand on it by writing a note about how each role makes you happy. (It would probably be easy to also list ways that each of those roles can make you unhappy, but that's not the exercise!)

Mom–not having messed up too badly yet

Manager–keeping the work flowing and meeting deadlines

Student-making sure I learn something every day

Lover-those knowing moments when you feel the underlying happiness of your relationship

Friend-maintaining friendships over time, even by e-mail

The point of this exercise is to try and increase the happiness you feel in these different roles. Write down positive steps you yourself can take to improve the satisfaction you receive from each role. This relates to the exercise in this book about identifying your strengths. You can draw on your strengths to improve the circumstances of the various roles you play. Whether your list contains big or small roles, you will begin to appreciate that you do feel a lot of happiness from the different roles you play in life.

_____

_____

_____

_____

_____

_____

_____

26) After a Vacation, Take Turns Making a List of 100 Moments You Remember (Big and Small), and Use This Method to Create Other Memory Lists for Other Occasions

When you come back from a vacation with a friend or loved one (or a group, like your family), create a list of 100 moments you remember. Each person takes turns, and every detail gets written down, no matter how small. The focus should be on the positive, on the funny, on the memorable. Without judgment or commentary, the moments recorded should be as close as possible to the actual experience. Editorializing or interpreting the moments is not the idea. The goal is to record pure experience from a shared vacation to another place.

taking a dryer sheet with you to keep your luggage fresh

Bristol, Rhode Island

a hot shower, washing your cares away

a sip of Riesling Trockenbeerenauslese

hearing a perfect rhyme

the first few seconds of warmth from a blazing fire

This type of memory list can be used for other occasions; holidays are a good example. With the sheer speed of modern life and our future-mindedness, we often do not take careful note of the present. Making a memory list is a way to savor an experience—a souvenir of the event that can be important to all involved, later reminisced about or shared with others. Think of your memory lists as photographs for the mind. When you review them, you will feel like you are looking at pictures of your vacations and special events.

_____

_____

_____

_____

_____

_____

27) Make a List of Who's in Charge of What at Home and Work to Reassure Yourself That Things Are Balanced

In a relationship or a family or any type of group, balance is often hard to achieve, especially when it comes to managing responsibilities. When things are out of balance, resentment and anger can build. It is important that we attempt to address this issue, taking into consideration the different persons' talents and strengths. To make the carrying out of these duties as efficient and pleasant as possible, these talents and strengths should play a part in the analysis so that balance may be achieved. Sometimes just being recognized for the things you do can be a source of great happiness.

Make a list of who is in charge of what tasks at home, and do the same for other areas, like your department or group at work. Do you notice an imbalance? Do you see someone's talents being wasted? Do you see opportunities to suggest changes, switches, or modifications that would increase everyone's happiness? Make notes on these and choose an appropriate time to share them.

Mom–work, dinners, dishes, grocery list, grocery shopping, paying the bills

Dad–work, laundry, yard work, car maintenance, kid chauffeuring

Kids–caring for family pets, taking out the garbage

---

28) Make a List of All Your Achievements (Big and Small), and Just Keep Adding to It

You may feel like a nobody, or you may see yourself as Superman/woman. But have you ever taken the time to make a list of your

accomplishments or achievements? Most of us have not, unless you want to count what is on your résumé. We all know that the résumé only tells the surface information. Not only are there many important underlying achievements, but there are also many more that we do not include on a résumé. It is great to be recognized for achievements by others, but your opinion of yourself is the most important one of all. No one can take that away from you.

Now is a great time to make a list of all your achievements, big and small, personal and professional. Keep adding to it. This exercise will help you recognize accomplishments as they come up. You will stop taking yourself for granted and start patting yourself on the back. Even adding little things to the list—like creating a delicious beef stroganoff or successfully clipping the cat's nails—will increase your pride. Reviewing your list can also be a source of inspiration for future achievements.

master's and PhD degrees
gave birth to children
saved some money
wrote more than thirty books, including one that sold 1 million
    copies
taught myself my profession

_____

_____

_____

_____

_____

_____

_____

29) Decide on a Subject You Are Really Interested In, and Start Writing Down Key Facts about It

Do you love learning new things? Did you love school, and have you always discovered opportunities around you to learn more? Something that will bring you happiness is making a list of key facts and other things you learn about a subject (or subjects) you are really interested in.

You will need a notebook devoted to this exercise. Picking the notebook and the subject will be a big part of the fun. The activity itself is an example of a way in which mental activity can produce enjoyment. The mind offers at least as many opportunities for action as the body. Studies have shown that it is extremely important for your well-being to keep the mind stimulated throughout your life. Studying things you want to learn about offers you the chance to understand what is happening around you and to develop a personally meaningful sense of what your experience is all about. You may be lucky enough to discover the flow of the mind's thinking and changes of attention. And it is amazing what a sense of control it gives to know that favorite facts are always at hand. Don't stop with one notebook. Continue this exercise with many subjects and notebooks. Inspire those around you to keep notebooks, too.

This activity is similar to what people did in old-fashioned commonplace books. People compiled these notebooks in the course of their readings in order to create a stock of ideas. They were a way to compile knowledge, usually by writing information into books. Commonplaces were used by readers, writers, students, and humanists as an aid for remembering useful concepts or facts they had learned.

Each commonplace book was unique to its creator's particular interests. Your notebook(s) should have that same feel.

_____

_____

_____

_____

_____

_____

_____

30) Make a List of Ways You Focus Attention Inward, and then Look for Ways to Focus on the World

When a person spends less time thinking about themselves, they find it easier to deal with stress. You can put a certain amount of focus on your own actions and take responsibility for them, but thinking about your own past and future puts you someplace else, and that someplace else does not help you or anyone around you. The present is the only time you are guaranteed to have.

Being totally focused on the present moment is powerful. It is looking outward from a calm center. Maybe you can focus on offering compassion to others; maybe you can provide loving-kindness; or maybe you can offer the gift of listening.

First, make a list of ways you habitually focus inward.

rehashing conversations

worrying about how I look

feeling sorry for myself when I am working and others are not

thinking about an ache or pain

planning what to ask someone

Then make a list of how you can focus outward, on the world and on others.

record a show for
    someone who
    is busy doing
    homework
volunteer on the library
    board
donate clothing to
    Goodwill
do nice things for oth-
    ers without saying
    anything about it
put catnip on the cat toy

When you work or study, focus entirely on the project at hand. Work toward not being carried away by *monkey mind*, that bunch of crazy thoughts that swing wildly back and forth in your brain, branching both logically and illogically. When you are performing a task, be right there paying attention to the details, the environment. Focus without judging these small acts. Both enjoyable and unenjoyable tasks will be completed with more efficiency and pleasure. Let your second list act as a set of reminders for happier living.

31) Don't Resist the Fun of a List; You Can Make a Game of Remembering Things in Order

What do you need for going to the beach? How many times do you run an errand to the store to pick up some items, and find you can't remember the entire list? Lists are practical, but they are also fun. This exercise is for the times when you cannot or do not want to write down a list. It is a brain exercise to find a way to keep a list in your head.

You could use mnemonics—using the initial letter of each item to create a sequence you memorize, thereby memorizing the items.

W(rite) an e-mail to a friend.

R(epot) the plants that have outgrown their containers.

F(ile) the photographs in albums.

You could envision a scene in detail where all the items are there. You could even prepare (and illustrate) a visual list in your brain, with open boxes for checking off items. You could repeat the list ten times in your head so that it is firmly planted in your memory.

It is fun to challenge yourself like this. Even if you do not accomplish all the items on your mental list, this type of challenge brings happiness.

32) Make a List of New Things to Talk About, Pursue, See, Visit, etc., for your Relationship

With every relationship, you must find ways to increase challenges and skills—like making an effort to talk about new topics, visiting new places, paying attention to the other's complexity. When relationships are new, this occurs naturally. So the longer the relationship is, the more important it is to do this. The unstinting investment is crucial to relationships. Make a list of ways you can do this, reminders you can use.

Maybe your only form of entertainment has been dinner and a movie. You could list other types of activities, including trying dinner and a movie in a totally different venue. In making the list, be sure to include what you want and need, but also, be sure to ask the other person what they would like to see on the list. Whether the list includes big or small things is not important. The making of this list is the important thing.

go see a Broadway play
discuss potential home
    improvements
visit a sports hall of fame
rake the leaves out of the garden
visit all the college towns in your state

_____

_____

_____

_____

33) Before You Go to Sleep, Make a List of Ten Things that Made You Feel Happy During the Day

What were the little things you noticed and the things that went right today? It is always good to stop and smell the roses. Making a list of the things that made you feel happy is often harder than rattling off the things that went wrong or which worry you. Why is that? Because we dwell too much on the negative—trying to "understand" or "figure it out," not following the simple rule that if you can't do something about it, let it go.

This exercise, if made a habit, will point you in the other direction. You will find that each day, you will pick up the positive more easily, and, later, remember it more readily. As happy events happen, you will be more aware of them. You can compare your life with the media. If you believe the media, more bad happens than good. If you believe your thoughts, more bad happens than good. This exercise is a "retraining" of your mind. Remember—although you think, you are not your thoughts. You can choose to focus on the positive and let the negative go. What better way to go to sleep than with the happy thoughts of your day.

    the flavor and aroma of Taster's
        Choice coffee
    the marbled endpapers in an
        antique book
    calm acceptance
    the simplicity of
        spaghetti
    the comfort of a cat

---

34) Make a List of Things You Have Faith and Trust In

Make a list of things you have faith and trust in, something you can stick in your wallet and take out when you need it. When you are feeling sad or spiritually lost, you can pull it out and read it over until you feel better.

First, you must look at your understanding of faith and trust. This is a very personal list because it deals with two very strong emotions. Having faith and trust in something can include a wide range of things. Nature is something you can have *faith* and *trust* in. How about breathing? How about yourself? Religion and spirituality also play a big part in this list—along with the fact that every single person seeks happiness. When you trust, you become centered, anchored.

This list is comforting, and teaches you to stop trying to control things. Use it to let go and trust in the natural flow of events and in life's ongoing changes.

My relationships are my teachers, my learning experience.

Humor rules over reason and hope.

Yoga is good for my mind and body.

There is a solution to every problem.

This too shall pass.

_____

_____

_____

_____

_____

35) Make a List of Things in Your Life that You Are Very Attached To

What things in your life are you very attached to?
What would happen if you let go of
one of them? Make a list, first of
all, of things you don't think
you can live without—
things you don't even
believe can be replaced.

> having coffee every
>   day
> watching television
> complaining
> surfing or e-shopping on the Internet
> reading magazines

What would happen if you let go of one, just for a day or a week?
Why not try that and see how it feels. Then try that for another item
on your list. You may be surprised at the results.

Instead of thinking about these things or spending time protecting or worrying about them, why not think about this: What could I do
right now that would bring me some lasting happiness? Could I call
a friend, finish a project, volunteer at a soup kitchen? Real happiness
is found inside, not with things.

_____

_____

_____

_____

_____

_____

36) Make a List of All the Sounds You Can Use as Mindfulness Bells

Make a list of all the sounds you can use as mindfulness bells. The mindfulness bell is the voice of our spiritual ancestors, Buddhist teacher Thich Nhat Hanh instructs: "Its sounds call us back to our true home in the present moment—to emptiness. We find peace, stability, freedom—the root of our happiness."

clocks
telephone
timer
doorbell
e-mail arrival
instant messages
car horn or siren
church bell
dog barking
cat meowing

Each time you hear or notice one, take three deep breaths, connecting with yourself and what you are doing.

When you hear the sound, you relax your body and become aware of your breathing. Once you have made a list of the sounds you hear regularly and then start practicing this exercise, you will relax naturally, with enjoyment. When you hear a mindfulness bell, you stop your conversation or whatever you are doing and bring awareness to your breathing. By stopping to breathe and restore your calm and peace, your work becomes more enjoyable and the friend in front of you becomes more real. With just three conscious breaths, you can release the tensions in your body and mind—and return to a clear, calm state of being.

_____

_____

_____

_____

_____

_____

37) List Ten Things You Can Do to Add Beauty to Your Life That Cost Little or No Money

The secret of happiness is that it is always a choice. We nurture our lives through the choices we make about where we live; the mood, spirit, and energy of our home; the food we eat, the rituals we perform, the clothes we wear; and the colors and items we select to uplift us. We cannot ignore the impact of the external world, but the art of life is in the living—not in the getting/collecting of more stuff. The difficult part is convincing yourself that it is just that easy to do.

You can make a list of ten things you can do to add beauty to your life, but this list should include only those things that cost little or no money. These little things can be as simple as oiling squeaky hinges so a door opens and closes better. Another could be lighting candles at dinnertime. As is often the case, the simplest things in life make us the happiest. Make this exercise a creative process.

love
bask in the sunlight
walk on the beach
be around children
savor your food
wear bright colors

38) Keep Lists of Words to Look Up in Dictionaries and Encyclopedias

Words fill our days. Whether we are a word nerd or a math enthusiast or somewhere in between, we can all appreciate words and language. As Noam Chomsky said, the most striking aspect of human linguistic competence is the "creativity" of language. It is our ability to produce new sentences—immediately understood by others—that is so amazing. We see new words all the time, and we also see familiar words about which we are curious. What's the origin of a term? How is it really pronounced? Is this word related or connected to that one?

big-box store

bracketology

coffee culture

nichification

wikiality

Learning about language, expanding your vocabulary, and improving your ability to communicate well are all things that bring us happiness. This exercise involves keeping a list (or lists) of words to look up in dictionaries or encyclopedias. This leads to knowledge and learning for the sheer fun of it.

_____

_____

_____

_____

_____

_____

39) Give a Friend a Top-Ten List of Reasons Why He or She Is Great

A lot of people are depressed because they are lonely. They do not have friends or do not cultivate the friendships they do have. We need to be part of a social world, however big or small. It does not matter if it is in your community (your town, in cyberspace, or scattered over the world). Who are your friends?

Pick one friend. Make a top-ten list of reasons why you think that person is great. Share this list with the person. It may sound dorky, but he or she will probably love it and cherish the list. This is just one way to cultivate a friendship. Each of us needs to experience a sense of social belonging.

patient
kind
hardworking
great father
compassionate son
good friend
great with Ideas
strong
willing to try new things
well-rounded

_____

_____

_____

_____

_____

40) Keep a List of Things You Want to Buy before Buying

How much of the hard-earned money you make gets thrown away on the temporary pleasure of buying something that immediately becomes assimilated into your ever-growing collection of "stuff"? Wouldn't that money be better used to pay down debt, or save for college or your retirement?

Keep a list of things you want to buy before buying. Then, once a week or once a month, test your memory of this list. If you forgot something was on the list and it is not something you absolutely need, cross it off.

When you are tempted to buy another pretty sweater (even though your closet is full of them), ignore the thought. Fluff up or rearrange your old sweaters so they seem new again. Don't buy so many magazines or look at every catalog that comes in the mail. Replace greedy thoughts with generous ones. Respect the imperma-nent nature of sweaters!

_____

_____

_____

_____

_____

_____

41) Throw Out Your Wish List and Be Happy with the Present Moment

This is an anti-list activity! You could take a leap of faith and either throw out or bury/hide your wish list. Instead of trying to think and plan everything out, dive into the present moment. The path to hap-piness is living each hour of the day in awareness, mind and body dwelling in the present moment.

Let there be no desire, and see what happens. There is no past, no future, no turmoil. You are content in the present moment. This is a big step toward inner peace.

42) Make a List of Ways to Share Joy with Others

What is joy to you? We often associate joy with the things and events in our lives that produce warm feelings of pleasure, but true joy requires no external stimuli. It is a state of mind that exists no matter what is happening around you. If you try, you can reflect your inner joy in your life and work. Bringing joy to others feeds your own happiness.

Look at joy as an unlimited supply that you can share and receive. It is your privilege to use your joy and to share it. Make a list of ways you can give/share joy with others. You can start with family members and friends, and then extend to the whole world.

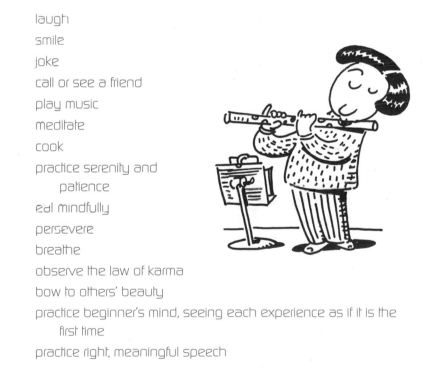

laugh

smile

joke

call or see a friend

play music

meditate

cook

practice serenity and
   patience

eat mindfully

persevere

breathe

observe the law of karma

bow to others' beauty

practice beginner's mind, seeing each experience as if it is the
   first time

practice right, meaningful speech

_____

_____

_____

_____

43) Make a List of Things You Most Enjoy but Typically Deny Yourself

Consider a list of things that you most enjoy but typically deny yourself—foods you prefer but have convinced yourself are bad for you; work breaks to relax and replenish your energy; little treats and presents. Start giving them back to yourself.

getting started later on work

taking a walk in the middle of the day, like just before lunch

ice cream

singing around the house

writing up things to be happy about

Although one of the major symptoms of depression is self-absorption, self-denial can pretty much work the same way. So, while some think "If I could only have a pint of ice cream today, I would feel happy"— there is the opposite camp that says, "If I never have ice cream or dessert, I will lose weight and feel happy." When this is presented in black and white, you can see that neither extreme works.

Remember that little pleasures may satisfy existing needs, help one achieve comfort and relaxation—but they do not produce change. That comes from activities that require skill and effort, that can offer gratifications, which produce flow. There's nothing wrong with little pleasures if you understand them as being just that—little. Real happiness is not quick and easy. Little pleasures can produce positive emotions, which may add to your motivation to create more flow and gratification.

_____

_____

_____

_____

_____

_____

_____

44) Make a List of the Five Most Memorable Experiences of Your Life, then Describe One and Try to Reawaken the Feelings

Savoring is an awareness of pleasure and the use of deliberate conscious attention applied to the experience of pleasure. Savoring is often used in the context of the present moment, but here we will use the technique with memories.

Make a list of five of the most memorable experiences of your life, which will likely be pleasant ones. Write up a list of the parts of each experience that you recall. By doing this, you may reawaken the feelings of such an experience. Take the opportunity to practice savoring by using one or more of the following five techniques:

> *Sharing with others*—telling others about the value of this
> experience for you
> *Memory-building*—by creating mental photographs or finding
> a souvenir from the event

Self-congratulation—works for some events where you
achieved something or you felt your good karma created
the outcome

Sharpening perceptions—closing your eyes and recalling the
details of sight, smell, taste, touch, and hearing that were
involved

Absorption—somewhat like daydreaming; just sensing and
immersing yourself in the memory

_____

_____

_____

_____

_____

_____

_____

_____

45) List Things That You Used to Have the Nerve to Do, and Write Down What You Would Need Now to Do Them Again

The strengths that make up courage include the exercise of will toward worthy ends that you are not certain
you can attain. Courage is doing something in the face of strong adversity,
against the odds. Courage is
perseverance and integrity.

Make a list of the
things you *used* to
do that you no longer
have the nerve or cour-
age to do. Try to figure out what
caused you to stop doing these

things. This understanding gives you tremendous insight into your feelings. Write down what you would need to do them now. What are you waiting for? Go for it!

travel via airplane
present talks at work
conferences
do consultant work
visit New York City
play music and sing

_____

_____

_____

_____

_____

_____

_____

_____

46) Trace Some of Your Favorite Things to Do Back to the Beginning, Your First Experience with Each

What are some of your favorite things to do? Make a list. Some-times it is helpful to trace your inspiration back to the place where an interest or hobby or vocation started. This exercise may help you create new passions.

I loved spelling tests in grade school. I was not a good student, but I could blow everybody else away on spelling tests. To pursue this in adulthood, I could take quizzes in spelling books, take online or interactive spelling tests, and even organize local spelling bees.

By going back to the origins of your favorite activities, you are digging down to your own personal foundation. We often lose sight of this in the busyness of life, but our core is really made up of our strengths and talents, which become manifest in the ideas, interests, and passions we choose to pursue. Maybe you have been on the wrong path, pursuing something you do not really like, or doing something for the wrong reasons. We have all heard stories about people who change their careers in order to do something they truly love, and perhaps we wonder if we have the courage to do the same thing.

Drilling to your core, to your basic self, can bring these passions to light. This may be a chance to reorient yourself toward happiness. Why not be one of those who continues to do their favorite things?

47) Make a List of What You Have Endured in Life That Has Made You Wiser

We have all faced bad news, unpleasant feelings, and true hardship. Like death and taxes, these feelings are inevitable in life. It is actually pretty easy to remember these things, so make a list. This is just the beginning of the exercise, however. The way to glean some happiness from this misfortune is to examine in what way(s) each of these events has made you a wiser person. We have all heard incredible stories of how people have overcome certain events in their lives. It is inspirational to hear their stories and the lessons they learned.

By accepting the directions your life takes, both good or bad, within or outside of your control, you accept life itself. Did any of these situations help you become more tolerant of others, more patient, more content with your life? In making this list, you will see that every event—trivial or life-changing, fortuitous or tragic—eventually ends. Things always change. Another important aspect of this exercise is that by reliving your reactions to bad news, unpleasant feelings, or true hardships again, you can have a delayed positive experience. Just because you did not learn something from the event when it happened, does not mean you cannot learn something from it now. In those times of crisis or disappointment, were you able to take away a positive lesson?

_____

_____

_____

_____

_____

_____

_____

48) Make Three Lists—How to Increase Your Awareness, Your Choices, Your Energy—Your Most Important Intentions

MAKE A LIST OF HOW TO INCREASE YOUR *AWARENESS*:

- Exercise awareness over your reactions to people you have an instinctive aversion to.
- Do tai chi for more bodily awareness.
- Transform chores into meditation by establishing and maintaining awareness while doing them.
- Listen to sounds and others' speaking with focused awareness.
- Work with creative awareness instead of on autopilot, being present in your thoughts and actions.

MAKE A LIST OF HOW TO INCREASE YOUR *CHOICES*:

- Develop a choiceless awareness of sensations, like sound.
- Stop in whatever situation you are in, long enough to understand that you have a choice about what to do or not do.
- The law of karma teaches that you have a choice in each new moment of what response your heart and mind will bring to the situation.
- Wake up to life, to all its choices and possibilities for change.
- Allow your choices to arise from the depths of your true nature, not your ideas about yourself.

MAKE A LIST OF HOW TO INCREASE YOUR *ENERGY*:

- Expend the bulk of your energy planting good "seeds" and "roots."
- Learn yoga poses that open and release your body, flooding it with life energy.

- Save energy by not getting irritated or angry, especially about things you cannot control.
- Eat enough to get energy, but not overfill.
- Learn breathing techniques for more energy and better health.

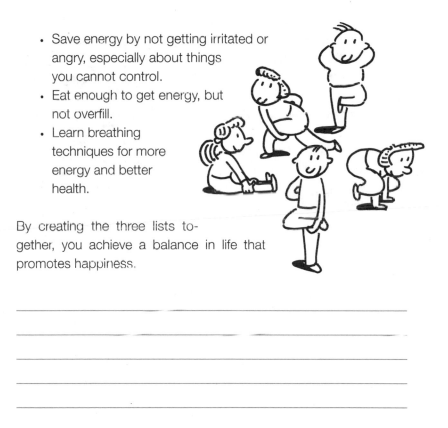

By creating the three lists to-gether, you achieve a balance in life that promotes happiness.

_____

_____

_____

_____

_____

_____

49) Make a List of Everything You Appreciate and Are Grateful For

The things you appreciate and are grateful for should be part of an ongoing list. Do not let anything get by you! These are the things that bring true happiness, mental contentment. (Mine's 100,000 entries long—too long to share in this field guide!)

Use this list, too. If there are people on it, take time to let them know how you feel—for example by sending them a letter of appreciation. If there is an organization on the list, let them know, too—or send a letter to the editor if it's for a group in your community.

Each day, pick something from the list or something you are about to add to the list, and share it with someone. Be thankful that you can appreciate what the day brings. Appreciate your state of continual "becoming." Each day, say, "I am awake and grateful to be alive."

Also, keep a list of compliments or thanks that you receive. You can go back over this list from time to time, recalling the words of appreciation you have received.

_____

_____

_____

_____

_____

_____

_____

50) Write Up Your Life as a List of Events, Stepping-Stones

Have you forgotten your school's colors in junior high and your third-grade teacher's name? How about the honors you have earned? It is good to take the time to write up your life as a series of events and stepping-stones. As time goes by and you do not revisit them, they can easily be forgotten. If you don't do it, who will?

Are there patterns? Do your list's stepping-stones focus on certain areas or places? Are these the areas that you see as the source of your happiness? Does the list make you proud? Does it inspire you? Are there new stepping-stones you are ready to add? Passion is what drives some people to the highest levels of accomplishment and beyond. This list can become an inspiration to you and to others when shared. How much don't your children know about you? How much don't you know about a parent or grandparent? By keeping a list of events and stepping-stones, you are offering inspiration to others who may read your list now and in the future.

---

51) List of Lists I

Here is a list of lists to make and then expand on. Look at this list and stop on an item that catches your attention, and feel free to add some of your own.

> achievements I am proud of
>
> adjectives describing myself
>
> answered prayers
>
> decisions I made that turned out well

jobs/careers I would like to have

lessons I have learned

marketing ideas for my business

my blessings

my skills

my talents

people I like to be with

people I want to forgive

people I want to forgive me

people I would like to meet

places I would like to visit

positive experiences I have had

possessions I am tired of owning

principles to live by

reasons I want to stay married/committed

things I am glad I have done

things I am grateful for

things I believe in

things I do well

things I have accomplished in my life

things I have to offer a partner/relationship

things I need or want to do

things I need to handle in order to have the highest integrity

things I should delegate

things I value in life

things I want my child to know about me

_____

_____

_____

_____

_____

_____

_____

52) List of Lists II

things I want to be remembered for
things I want to do before I die
things I want to tell my mother/father
things I will never do again
things I would do if I had six months to live
things I would do if I had time
things I would do if I were the person I admire
things I would like to hear
things I would like to tell my child
things I would save if the house were on fire
things that are going right
things that make me laugh
things that nourish me
things that once scared me but do not anymore
things that turn me on
things to do when I am alone
things to do when I feel depressed
things to forgive myself for
things/people/places I love
times I have been acknowledged
times I have been right, how I knew it, and what I did
times I have felt creative
times I have felt fulfilled

ways I am like someone I admire

ways I can make money

ways I could nurture myself

ways I help others

ways in which I am generous

what I like about myself

what I want to add to my life

what I want to eliminate from my life

_____

_____

_____

_____

_____

_____

_____

PART 2: MIND-MAPPING

Mind maps can be used to work with thoughts and feelings, to work out solutions to issues and problems with happiness as the goal. There has been much written about using mind maps to assist learning, remembering, and organizing—but less about how to use mind mapping for problem solving, self-analysis, and the achievement of happiness. Mind maps can be an aid to unlock creative thinking or clarify emotions. This part of the book shows how mind maps can be used to give readers a greater insight into their needs, desires, and goals—using self-analysis and problem solving to achieve happiness.

53) Mind-Mapping Your Favorite Word

Think hard about what your favorite word is. It could be your favorite because of the way it sounds or because of its connotations or because it represents something that you want or which regularly makes you feel happy. Or it could be a word that you heard someone use and for some reason remains with you.

Remember Wilfred J. Funk's "Most Beautiful Words in the English Language"? They were:

tranquil, golden, hush, bobolink, thrush, lullaby, chimes, murmuring, luminous, damask, cerulean, melody, marigold, jonquil, oriole, tendril, myrrh, mignonette, gossamer, fawn, dawn, chalice, anemone, mist, oleander, amaryllis, rosemary, camellia, asphodel, and halcyon.

Is it possible that he found these words to be lovely just as much for their meanings and associations as for their sounds? Note that Dr. Funk's list is filled with birds and flowers.

You will need a pen. Put your favorite word in the middle of the blank part of this page and fill in quickly, with printed single key words on the lines and without pausing to choose, the first ten associations that radiate from the center when you think of the original concept. It is important to put down the *first* words that come into your mind, no matter how ridiculous they may seem. This exercise is not a test and should take you no more than a minute. By performing the exercise, you can experience an instant explosion in mental power and optimism.

---

54) Mind-Mapping a Five-Year Plan

Many books refer to creating a five-year plan. Five-year plans help you achieve the goals that are important to you and that create happiness. Planning is an important aspect of experiencing happiness. It acts as a guide for you. Instead of a list, which is linear, let's try a mind map for this exercise. Start with the center being NOW and branch off seven ways, using single-word or short-phrase descriptions of your life as it is now. The seven lines will describe these aspects.

Then, branch to the next five years off each of these rays, i.e., your description of your health will branch to a year from now, two years from now, three, four, and then five years from now. Don't spend too much time seeking an answer to how you foresee your progress. Write in what comes to mind, what seems logical, reasonable, natural, and attainable. As with many things in life, a little planning can go a long way.

55) Mind-Mapping Your Ideal Day

Start with a colored image in the center that represents your ideal day. An image is often worth a thousand words and can encourage creative thought. An ideal day does not have to be a day off from work or a weekend day. It can be a day at work or school. From there, write down everything that comes to mind, making a branch for each significant thought. Print the words and add images while you go, or when you run out of thoughts that easily come to mind. Use colors for the thoughts if you like.

In creative efforts like this, the mind should be left as "free" as possible to come up with what goes on the branches of the mind map. The idea is to write down everything your mind thinks of around a central idea.

Now look at the mind map. Does it resemble a day you have ever had? Often had? Never had? What are the reasons for your answer? What can you do to create your ideal day in real life? What is the highest-priority item that is missing from your life right now? Do you have ideal days when you are on vacation? If you have a single resounding answer to this question, you've got your target.

56) Mind-Mapping an Important Goal from Step One

What is a goal? A goal is the basic unit of life design. It is easy to dream, but if you want to make that dream come true, you will have to start by choosing what you are going to go for first. This is usually the most challenging aspect of this exercise. It can be a difficult process to determine what your goals are. It does take practice. To do this exercise, remember that, first, a goal is concrete. It is a set of facts. You will know when you have arrived. Say the goal is "get a PhD." This is a goal that has concrete steps and an end date. The date is as important as selecting the target and knowing the steps. The second step in this process is to say, "This is what I want," even if it is for now. No goal is set in stone or written in blood. Remember that goals exist to serve you and make you happy.

So, choose a goal that is important to you. Diagram the steps as you know them. Are you ready to take the first step? Think of this as a "trial project." Take that first step and see how you like this. If you feel good, really good, about it—continue!

---

57) Idea-Mapping to Increase Creativity

Pick an object, like a piece of fruit. Write down what it is. Do you see an image? Is there color in the image? How quickly did you get an image and what was it? Now, what are the associations around the image?

As you can see, the image was stored in your mind. You simply needed to trigger its release. Mind-mapping involves imagination and association, and it can be a great tool for jump-starting creativity. First, branch out the preparatory steps. Then take a break. Let the mind gather energy. Come back to the mind map when you have had an Aha! moment related to the original idea, and continue to map out

more associations and connections, potentially illuminating your path. Be sure to include all the reasons you can do something and all the reasons it will work. Delay any judgment. Have fun and enjoy your creativity.

_____

_____

_____

_____

_____

_____

_____

_____

58) Mind-Map Meditation (Following Monkey Mind)

The mind is usually caught up in anxious thought construction and thought projection, jumping around like a monkey or squirrel from branch to branch to branch. You probably do not realize how pervasive this is in your own mind. A mind-map meditation will help you concentrate on your meditation. This exercise starts with the middle of a large piece of blank paper. Close your eyes in meditation and focus on your breath. A writing instrument should be in your hand, or handy.

Watch the breath where it goes in and out of the nostrils and focus on the rise and fall of the chest and abdomen. Soon, a thought will arise because the mind has wandered off. Write it in the center. This is a different type of mind map, so don't worry at all about the design. Close your eyes again and go back to the breath. When the mind wanders off again (and it will!), write down where it went — words, images, sounds. Don't worry about how many times the mind wanders and you have to return to focus on the breath. After five to twenty minutes of this, have a look at what you have written down. By learning how to focus your mind in meditation, you will slowly achieve calm and happiness.

---

59) Idea-Mapping a Book You Want to Write, a Song or Artwork You Want to Create

We each have something in mind that we want to create. Do you want to paint or write a song or pen a novel? Maybe you have something more complicated in mind. From the simplest creation to the more complicated ones, a first step is needed to begin to achieve a creative goal. An idea-mapping exercise gives you the necessary foundation to begin your work.

You can use an idea map to cobble out the steps toward achieving your creative goal. In the center of your idea map, write what you want to create. Branch off all the pieces of the project. This idea map will help you get started. Doing something like this for yourself is a big happiness booster.

_____

_____

_____

_____

_____

_____

60) Mind Map for Assessing a Situation's Advantages and Disadvantages

To help with a decision, you can create a mind map of the advantages (pros) and disadvantages (cons) of this situation. What could go wrong? What are the potential benefits? It takes time and thought to write down all the possibilities.

While the mind map does not make the choice for you, it will dramatically increase your ability to make the right choice by highlighting the key trade-offs. In many cases, the process of mind-mapping itself generates your best choice. The brain gets an overview of all the data and, if you're lucky, there is an Aha! moment.

If, after completion of the mind map, your decision is still not clear, a number-weighting method can be used. Each key word on the mind map can be assigned a number from 1 to 100 according to its importance. Again, if this does not resolve the matter, you might want to meditate on this mind map, let it incubate in your brain. If nothing else, you will reach a point where your intuition or gut will tell you which way to go.

_____

_____

_____

_____

_____

_____

61) Create a Mind Map for Staying "On Task"

Do you find that there are certain activities that you put off, procrastinate about, start but have trouble finishing, or start but constantly
abort? In other words, do you have trouble staying "on task" during
certain projects? If so, it would be helpful to make two mind maps.

The next time the activity or project comes into play, map out
what happens. While you are doing online research, do you pop over
to shopping sites to browse? When you are supposed to be writing a
report, do you toddle off for coffee or a snack? Write down the series
of events so you can see how numerous the interruptions are. Just
being aware of the many interruptions will help you stay on task and
focused. When you become more efficient at completing certain projects, the process may become more enjoyable because it does not

take as long to com-
plete as before.

Then make a mind
map for ideally carry-
ing out the activity or
project with the fewest
interruptions. Do you
think you would feel
happier if you used this
second mind map?

_____

_____

_____

_____

_____

_____

_____

62) Take One Great Idea You Have Not Pursued and Mind-Map How You'd Ideally Pursue It If You Had the Means

Maybe you would like to achieve more in business or life in general. You have a great idea, but are either unsure of how to pursue it, or know how and do not have the means available to follow through.

Start with your idea in the middle of the page. To one side, write the steps you are sure must be taken and what the goal of each is. Use colors or drawings to denote which items you cannot do because of a resource you do not have, but also mark those you could go ahead with.

On the other side, write your questions. Write down the parts that puzzle you. Make notes on where (or with whom) you might start to get help with these questions. Feel free to share this exercise with other people. You never know when someone else may agree that your idea is great and have the resources you need to help you accomplish your goal. Many major advances in science have come through the sharing of knowledge.

_____

_____

_____

_____

_____

_____

_____

_____

63) Mind-Map Something You Have Never Seen into Parts You Have Experienced to Realize How You Can Use Your Mind to Alter Your Experience and Expand Your World

What is something you have never actually seen? A whale? The Eiffel Tower? For this mind map, you might supplement the activity by looking up the entity in a dictionary and/or encyclopedia. What parts of a whale have you seen on another creature? Mouth, fin, eyes, tail? Maybe you have seen a dolphin, so you have seen a blowhole. Make a mind map of all these parts, adding some description or even a drawing.

Have you seen the lattice-arch span of a bridge? This type of iron construction makes up the base of the Eiffel Tower. Have you seen a prefabricated house? That is how the Eiffel Tower was built. All of the tower's 12,000 pieces were prefabricated off-site and assembled with precision down to the last fraction of an inch. Write up a mind map of parts—legs, open-lattice sides, two flat floors, even a

meteorology station—that you have seen before. Now you can sense what it would be like to experience the Eiffel Tower. Many people visit it but do not really see its details—but you can!

_____

_____

_____

_____

_____

_____

_____

_____

64) Mind-Map to Improve Your Perception of a Situation, Even When You Cannot Directly Influence What Happens

Looking at a situation with full awareness and alertness can help you improve your perception of it. Most of us react emotionally, especially with situations we cannot control or even influence. We feel helpless, and thus, we may feel depressed, sad, or even angry.

By creating a mind map of a situation, you can look at what is truly going on. You are stopping to look at this one thing. Try to examine the causes. Be realistic about the effects. Look at motivations and intentions. Is some compassion arising? Are resentment and anger disappearing?

Can you change your perception now? Your aim is to reach a perception that creates well-being, not more suffering.

_____

_____

_____

_____

_____

_____

_____

_____

65) Rewirc Your Brain: First, Make a Mind Map of How You Would Usually Handle a Situation; then, One of How You Can Change That to a Happier, More Positive Reaction

You can learn a lot about yourself and others by the way you/they handle a rainy day, lost luggage, or tangled Christmas lights. Make a mind map of how you would usually handle one or more of these situations. Be honest—brutally so.

Now, branch off of the mind map, changing reactionary or negative steps into happier, more positive responses. The point is to stop and think—am I alleviating a bad situation or causing more suffering? Everyone can develop a flexibility of response. In the face of an unhappy situation, one can practice patience, compassion, gratitude. When this type of thinking becomes more natural, you will see that whenever an unpleasant situation arises, you will be able to handle it in a more positive way. The law of karma tells you that you have a choice in each new moment of what response your heart and mind will bring to your situation.

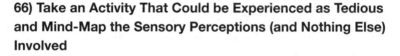

_____

_____

_____

_____

_____

_____

_____

_____

_____

_____

66) Take an Activity That Could be Experienced as Tedious and Mind-Map the Sensory Perceptions (and Nothing Else) Involved

Is there something you dread doing? Do you wonder why you have to carry out this tedious task so often? Is it getting ready in the morning, or the drive/ride to work, or paying the bills? Take an activity you view as tedious and prepare a mind map—not of the steps involved, but of your own sensory perceptions. Why do you dread this activity so much? We often look at such tasks as a burden or annoyance. By breaking the activity down in a very different way, can you see it from another perspective? Is there a way to find enjoyment in the struggle?

There is a lot of routine in life, and sometimes we feel like we are on a hamster wheel. The routines seem dull and meaningless. By looking at these routines, maybe you can also make changes. If something is done habitually at a certain time or in a certain way, change the routine to a ritual. A ritual is something to look forward to rather than dread. The ritual is full of the excitement of the unknown. By taking a different route home from work, do you get to see a part of your town that you are not familiar with? Instead of using regular bread in the sandwiches you make every morning, make wrap sandwiches to make them more exciting. Any small change can make a big (happy!) difference in your perception.

_____

_____

_____

_____

_____

_____

_____

67) Get a Big Roll of White Butcher Paper or Post-it Sticky Board and Place It on the Wall for Brainstorms, Inspiration Storms, Idea Storms

Making mind maps can be an art, no matter what the topic is. You can create them on rolls of white butcher paper. You can post them on a wall, bulletin board, or Post-it sticky board. Butcher paper is better than conventional paper because it is less expensive; plus, it is big and dramatic. Writing mind maps or lists on a wall with this paper can force your maps to evolve and become pure inspiration. You can use this technique to help you solve problems, or to help you become more creative with many aspects of your life. It does not matter

what you use this technique for; you will find it useful and achieve a different perspective than you normally would. Having this large amount of paper available, you will find that you start to use it intuitively to make notes and lists into maps that become an invaluable and indispensable part of your life.

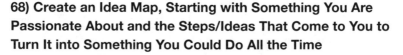

68) Create an Idea Map, Starting with Something You Are Passionate About and the Steps/Ideas That Come to You to Turn It into Something You Could Do All the Time

What are you passionate about? What do you like to spend most of your free time doing? Is there a new hobby that you would like to take up? Do you think about it a lot, dreaming about getting started? This can be the most difficult part: being brutally honest with yourself when it comes to finding your passion. Most people have dreams in their minds but they never intend to act upon them because they are afraid of the dream dying. This exercise is designed to take that fear away. Find your passion and idea-map it out. Hopefully, you will have the courage to find many things you are passionate about and to ultimately pursue them through this idea-mapping exercise.

This idea map starts from that passion. Radiate the steps, ideas, and projects from that center. Then start another branch that describes how you could turn this passion into something you do all the time. What would it take? Would there be risks or major roadblocks? How could you do more of what you like to do? The more you challenge yourself—mentally, physically, and emotionally—the more gratification you will experience. Find your passion and make it part of who you are.

_____

_____

_____

_____

_____

_____

_____

_____

_____

69) Mind-Map a Number of Possible Affirmations in the Present Tense That Would Be Effective for You

In the center of a mind map, write the goal, which is how you want to feel—maybe "I am happy." From this, branch out, writing affirmations that you believe would be effective for you.

I am a seed, sprouting anew.

I rest in tranquility.

I am calm and centered.

I am fulfilled and happy.

Maybe you can use qualities you really like or would like to have. These can be stated as affirmations.

I am a good person.
I am kind.
I am patient.
I trust myself and others.

Use this mind map to meditate on your ideals. Just thinking about affirmations that are important to you will have a positive effect on you. Pick one off the map to use for the day. Pick one to repeat on your walk or during your commute. Use the affirmations, then let go.

_____

_____

_____

_____

_____

_____

_____

_____

_____

70) Mind-Map Something You Really Need to Express but Are Having Trouble With (Forgiveness, a Request, an Expression of Love or Thanks)

We think a lot about things we want to say, we meant to say, we need to say. It is good to have a filter, to not blurt everything out. It is good to consider timing and whether what you have to say will be beneficial or harmful.

Make a mind map for a situation like this. You want to forgive someone; you have a request that is difficult to make; you want to express your love or thanks. Whatever it is, write down what has been holding you back. Plan how to say it, when to say it, and even examine whether or not it should be said. Look at your intentions and motivations. Be gentle. Relax. Then express yourself. What you say, and just saying it, can be one of the greatest gifts you give to yourself and others.

_____

_____

_____

_____

_____

_____

_____

_____

71) Mind-Map the Word *Happiness*

Through a brainstorming exercise, you will discover the potential of your associative machinery, as well as some insight into your individuality. Fill in quickly, with single key words printed on the lines, and without pausing to choose, the first ten associations that radiate from the center when you think of the concept of happiness. It is important to put down the first words that come into your mind, no matter how ridiculous they may seem. This should take about a minute total. This exercise can be completed more than once, because your life, mood, and awareness constantly change over time. What you brainstorm on one day may be quite different from what you brainstorm on another day a month later.

From this one word and one exercise, you can see that any word or sensation is a tiny center, with potentially thousands or millions of associations emanating from it. When you complete this exercise with another person (or a group), you can also see that the associations you wrote down are magically different from what another person would write. Look at the associations you made to the word *happiness*. What do they say about you? What are the obvious patterns? Do you have control over many of the associations, or do you feel that they are out of your control?

_____

_____

_____

---

72) Mind-Map the Happy People, Places, and Objects in Your Life with Colorful Pictures and Drawings

Make a colorful, inspirational mind map of the people, places, and maybe even some objects that make you feel the happiest—maybe even photographs, pictures cut out of magazines, and your own drawings. This is a snapshot of your life right now, a positive one. You can keep adding to this mind map—or post it "as is" to remind you of how sweet life is. This exercise lets you use another creative outlet to understand your life and figure out what makes you feel happiest.

This exercise can be repeated annually, maybe around the time of your birthday.

---

73) Map Out Mistakes You Have Made That You Can Now Deem Acceptable and Even Enjoyable Parts of the Learning Process

How much suffering do you experience due to regret or second-guessing the choices and decisions you have made? And as the number of options increases, do you notice you feel worse about whatever you choose? One way to find more happiness is to stop trying to make the perfect choice. Another way is to commit to not second-guessing yourself.

Here's where the mind map comes in. Write down a mistake (or a few) that you have made. Consciously focus on the good aspects of the choice you made. The more you appreciate and enjoy the choice you did make, the less regret you will experience. Remember how complex life is and realize how rare it is that any single decision has the life-changing power we sometimes ascribe to it. We usually try to make the best decisions that we can with the information we have at the moment. Sometimes this just does not work out for us at the time. In reality, you did the best you could; you had no concrete idea of where your choice(s) would lead. To be happy, drop the words "if only" and substitute "next time." Beating yourself up does not create any positive feelings.

_____

_____

_____

_____

_____

_____

74) Mind-Map to Express Your Idea of the Ideal Job

Thomas Edison said, "I never did a day's work in my life. It was all fun." What is your ideal job? Mind-map it all out: the actual work, the hours, the type of boss/management structure, education needed, vacations, money, etc. This is an important point, seeing that you spend a lot of time working. How can you enjoy your job as much as possible? Do you have the skills or strengths to attain what you want? If not, can you acquire those skills and strengths? Make sure to include not just what you want from the job, but what you can/would contribute and produce. Is this ideal job something you can work toward and achieve? Save this information and use it on your résumé and on job interviews to help you secure your ideal job.

Alternatively, can you find positive ways to view and deal with your present job? Make a mind map of ways that you can do your job with your whole heart, finding delight in doing it. If your current job or career is not your ideal job, then it is important to find the positive aspects of the position while you figure out your true calling. Can you be "in the moment" of every task, paying close attention, infusing it with awareness, not wishing to be somewhere else? Write down ways to use work as a vehicle for spiritual and emotional growth.

_____

_____

_____

_____

_____

_____

_____

75) Make Mind Maps for Why It Would Be Fun to: Go Out with, Buy a, Learn a, Change a, Believe a, Withdraw from a, Begin a, Create a, Finish a ~

Mind maps can be used for wishes, and as a concrete way to work out the reasonableness of a wish. Maybe it would be fun to buy a fake-fur coat, learn how to make pizza from scratch, finish a crossword puzzle, etc. Pick a wish, big or small, and put it in the center.

Put all the reasons it would "be fun to" do this, radiating them from the center. Are you also thinking about some downsides? You might want to note those, for at the end of this exercise you want to either be inspired to start or to have decided the wish should step aside for another that would be more fun.

_____

_____

_____

_____

_____

_____

_____

_____

_____

76) Create a Mnemonic Mind Map with Wake-Up Calls and Mindfulness Bells Tied to the Cues

Life can be happier and more satisfying when we do our best to make it so. It has less to do with the external world and depends much more on our internal state. We have much more control over our internal state than we have over the external world. When we realize that the internal state we have is within our control, it becomes a powerful force. In this exercise, you create a wake-up call, a set of five to seven items that you can memorize as a personal mnemonic for happiness.

After choosing yours, make sure you use either the first letter of the first word or some other letter so you can turn the set into a series of letters you can memorize.

Wake up!
Breathe
Listen
Moderation
Patience
Stop

_____

_____

_____

_____

_____

_____

_____

_____

77) Put Together an Idea Map of New and Unique Ways to Achieve Happiness alongside Preexisting or Past Memories

Make a list of the ways you usually seek what you call "happiness." Just pick ten favorites, your most often used and most available methods:

watch a favorite TV show
listen to music

practice yoga
eat a pint of ice
    cream
read a magazine

Then, think outside your box. What are some new things you could try? What are some unique methods that may bring happiness? How about:

go on a media fast
read an encyclopedia article
walk in the rain
take up kayaking
perform a Japanese tea ceremony
decide not to answer the phone

Expand your list even further by picking a few events that need a partner or partners to do. Do you see how even your happiness boosters may be in a rut? Your happiness state will only change if you do things differently and if you increase the number of happiness "habits" you develop. Expanding your happiness horizons is an ideal way to increase the number of chances you have to be happier.

_____

_____

_____

_____

_____

78) Solving a Personal Behavioral Problem

In the middle of a piece of paper, put a behavioral problem you have—like impatience or reactiveness—and then do a mind-map burst, with all the thoughts and emotions triggered by the idea, including the root causes. Then create a second mind map working out a specific plan of action to solve it.

It could help to look at how you handle your relationships, your approach and attitude toward money, how your behavior at work affects things, and what you do that impacts your physical health and well-being—and that of those people close to you.

This exercise is about taking responsibility for your own actions and the way you respond to situations that you experience in your daily life. It is really important to understand what type of person you are if you feel you need to change certain behaviors in yourself. Try to see yourself as others see you. You are more in control of what happens to you than you think. You own the consequences of your behaviors, and what you choose to do or not do will directly impact your state of happiness.

_____

_____

_____

_____

_____

_____

_____

79) Interpersonal Problem Solving

To solve interpersonal problems, you could try doing three mind maps for likes, dislikes, and then solutions for the relationship. The two people involved can do this exercise together, and then present the mind maps to each other in an attempt to agree on solutions. See how many common solutions there are in the mind maps.

The people involved may want to set some ground rules. The intent is to improve the relationship, thereby increasing everyone's happiness. Keep the personal stuff like name-calling and insults out of it. There is no room for this type of attitude when trying to find solutions to interpersonal problems. So the "dislikes" need to be well thought out, and the person compiling them needs to consider whether what is being included will be helpful or just hurtful. Always err on the side of trying to be helpful. You will be surprised by how much can be accomplished and solved when you are honest with another person and attempt to work things out together.

_____

_____

_____

_____

_____

_____

_____

80) Mind-Map Diary

You can create a mind-map diary with yearly plans, monthly plans, and daily plans divided into these categories: family and friends, creativity, work, and health. You can also do a retrospective record of events, combined with images. Using color and illustrations or pictures can be inspirational.

A mind-map diary makes sense for anyone who enjoys a more graphic/visual approach to planning or record-keeping. Determine if you are this type of person, as this knowledge will be useful for many activities in this book, and throughout your life.

_____

_____

_____

_____

_____

_____

_____

81) Mind-Mapping to Remember

If you find that your inability to remember things bothers you, try mind-mapping to remember names, trivia, jokes, and other things that will improve your relationships and communications.

The multiple dimensions of a mind map will dramatically improve your memory skills by creating an internal three-dimensional image that uses associations, color, and time. This type of mind map can assist your recall of a story, plot, dream, family event, or even a to-do list. One particularly useful application is searching for a "lost" memory—perhaps a person's name or the whereabouts of an object.

You can leave the center of the mind map blank and surround it with words and images associated with the absent center. Think of it like putting together a jigsaw puzzle. Each word and image is a piece of the puzzle. When the mind map triggers the memory, and you solve the puzzle, you gain confidence, mental functioning, and motivation. This ability adds to one's overall happiness and sense of well-being.

_____

_____

_____

_____

_____

_____

_____

82) Catching Your Dreams

Although we have dreams all night, we do not always remember them in the morning. Dreaming and daydreaming are great when it comes to setting your imagination free.

Mind maps are the perfect way to help you catch your dreams. The more you can remember, the more you will enrich your imagination and memory. Keep a pen/pencil and pad next to the bed. When you go to bed, spend a minute or two thinking about dreaming. Repeat to yourself, "I will remember my dreams."

When you wake up in the morning, resist jumping out of bed. Try to lie still and even stay sleepy. The best time to remember your dreams is

when you first wake up. What is rolling about in your head? Is there an image? feeling? words? As you lie still, bits of your dreams may start to come back. Grab the pad and write down anything you can remember. Drawing the mind map may help jog your memory even more.

Keep the dream mind maps to see if there is a pattern to your dreams. You can learn a lot about yourself by remembering and interpreting your dreams. The unconscious and subconscious mind can solve many problems for you.

---

83) Exploring Patterns

Use mind-mapping to allow your mind to explore patterns, like a pinball machine. Everywhere around you there are patterns, cycles, sequences, and hierarchies. Recognizing and remembering patterns and the order of things can be very helpful and add to your happiness. Noting patterns helps you understand how much your world is made up of these. This mind-map exercise involves imagination and association to aid your memory.

You could also turn this around and make the exercise more about recognizing patterns than remembering them. Do you know the steps of various processes you perform? In your job, are there things that you know about "the way things work" or "how things happen"? Patterns also appear in the everyday instructions we follow to keep life moving smoothly.

Have fun with this mind-map exercise. Much of what is called "intelligence" is our ability to recognize order in the form of patterns. What patterns do you detect? Can you use them to better understand your life, and life in general?

_____

_____

_____

_____

_____

_____

_____

_____

84) Information Holding Spot

Mind-mapping keeps information in play, allowing us to make new connections and bounce off other ideas to make new ideas. When you get an idea down on paper, it frees the mind to go on to other ideas with the security of knowing that your idea is now written down. The information is now available to you anytime you wish to review or analyze it.

Much of our thinking is associative. One idea makes you think of another—no matter how logical/illogical the connection. Without forcing things, get an idea down on paper. Here, you set it free. What hunches have you had lately? How can you apply them to your idea?

To create new ideas, you need the materials from which they are made: facts, concepts, knowledge, experiences, feelings, and whatever else you can find. The more divergent your sources, the more original the idea you create is likely to be. Use this mind map to capture and develop flashes of insight when they occur. After the first mind-map "burst," be sure to come back and reconstruct and revise. The short break will allow your brain to integrate ideas generated in the burst. Then you can make a new mind map in which you identify the major branches or ideas before you combine, categorize, and find new connections.

85) To-Do Lists

Mind-mapping your to-do lists and goals makes it a flexible process. Using colors, maybe even large pieces of paper, you can create an instant view of where you are and where you are going. The color you choose for "finished" gives you a sense of success or reward.

Instead of standard, similar-looking lists, why not make the process more fun and useful? This type of to-do list may provide the extra inspiration you need to complete your task. A to-do list can involve items of varying priority, place (some in the house, some in the office, some outside errands), type (phone, e-mail, physical activity), etc. A mind map can be used to separate these into categories that make such a list more fun and intuitive to carry out. The connections and associations made will be useful the next time you need to assemble a list of things to do. You will more readily see the associations and find you are better organized. I guarantee that if you create a to-do list in this fashion and someone sees it, he/she will ask you questions about it. It gives you an opportunity to inspire someone else.

You can make this map a real working tool by adding phone numbers, appointment times, and e-mail addresses, too.

_____

_____

_____

_____

_____

_____

_____

86) Garbage Writing

Try garbage writing, an exercise where you let the words flow onto the paper without trying to make sense of them. Garbage writing means what it says: You simply pour out all the useless noise going on in your mind (a veritable smorgasbord) and get rid of everything that is distracting you from focusing.  It's like taking out the trash in your head, easy and very therapeutic — just dump it all on a page and get it out of your way.

Doing this on a mind map is helpful because every item is on a different branch. In this case, you are not looking for associations or structure. It is a method for working on your subconscious, which is preoccupied with these distractions.

Set a time limit of five, ten, or fifteen minutes, and just write. Anything that pops into your head, just write it down. Even if you think, "I cannot think of anything"—write that down!

The exercise brings you into, out of, around, and completely away from ideas. Looking at it afterwards, you will be surprised. It may be a nice plump "turkey" just waiting to be carved into new ideas and activities.

_____

_____

_____

_____

_____

_____

_____

_____

87) Interests, Hobbies, Skills, Talents

Mind-map your interests and hobbies as well as your skills and talents. To this, you can add the skills and talents you need and want to develop.

There is an equal chance, depending on the kind of person you are and where you're at in life, that you will have a full, impressive list or one that looks sparse. Our interests and hobbies tend to ebb and flow, often depending on our commitments and responsibilities, both at work and at home. However, your skills and talents do tend to grow and accumulate through life experience. So, make four major branches and write down what you know from the heart.

You may see some intersections. A topic in the back of your mind might come forward as a result and you can add it to your "interests" branch.

This map is one to keep coming back to—for inspiration, things to do, motivation, and growth toward more happiness. Even if you cannot accomplish any activities now, you have created a useful list for the future.

88) Mind-Map Your Ideal Future

Why not? It can't hurt to daydream a little. You can mind-map an ideal future for yourself, and use it to really consider whether you would be happier if things worked out this way. Do you think that attaining these items will ensure your happiness? Is there the possibility that once attained, a whole new set of desires would take their place?

Consider also the possibility of staying in the present moment and deeming it "ideal." You may be able to rattle off troubles, problems, and examples of suffering—but how can you appreciate beauty if there is no ugliness, or joy if there is no sadness, or good health if there is no illness? How about appreciating life knowing there is also death? What are you waiting for? While it is always wise to live in the present moment, it can also be prudent to spend a little time and effort planning for the future. You can choose to be happy in your ideal life this very minute.

_____

_____

_____

_____

_____

_____

_____

_____

89) Your Life

Make a mind map that resembles an actual road map, jigsaw puzzle, or giant game board—of your life.

Make this exercise—the game of LIFE—really creative and funny. Life *is* funny, especially when you think of it in these terms: You are born and then you die, and in the middle, all kinds of funny things happen to you. Life just lends itself to this type of creative activity. The connections are not important—just pick out events, accomplishments, mistakes, places, things, and people that have been part of your journey. Create a road map, jigsaw puzzle, game board, or

montage/collage of everything—whichever one appeals most to you. Don't try to do this in one sitting. The longer it takes you to complete it, the more meaningful it will be to you. Keep it fun.

_____

_____

_____

_____

_____

_____

_____

90) Mind-Map a Major Decision You Are Facing

The more you look at a situation in detail, the better prepared and the more flexible you will be in tackling it. In every major decision there is some "bad" and some "good," as well as some unknown territory that represents a new opportunity that will provide food for thought. Most decisions are not black and white, but gray.

The fascinating elements are those observations and questions that you can ponder and build on for the future. These can help you determine your way forward. By completing this exercise, you are forced to concentrate on the decision and practice a little patience— two very important elements in decision making, because you are trying to make the best possible decision that you can based on the information available to you.

First of all, imagine: If I did X, what is the worst that can happen? When? Where? Fill this part in on a mind map.

Then ask yourself: If I did X, what would be positive about the situation? Fill in the words on another mind map.

The next step is to combine these elements on a mind map with the question in the middle. Use this as a practical working tool to maintain an optimistic perspective in decision making. After your decision is made, document what worked and what you learned from your mind map for future use.

---

91) Mind-Map Your Vision/Mission in Life (Right Now)

Your vision or mission in life is a higher level of purpose, inspired by a personal set of life goals. These may be meant for you, or for society at large. Achieving them or just working toward them brings a great deal of lasting happiness and satisfaction.

For some, the dream is something they have always known. These people have not had to sit down and work out what it is that drives them and gives their lives meaning. If this describes you, documenting your vision or mission in life on a mind map will help keep you organized and focused on your journey.

Others need to approach this task more consciously. Some

people need practice at thinking about life in these terms because they have not yet been exposed to this type of philosophy. Taking the first step is very exciting and can create a mountain of happiness for you to experience. Start a mind map and write down any goals that are clear to you. Think of someone you admire, someone who is able to do what it is you find hard to put your mind to. Add detail to the goals, working toward renewing a sense of purpose and enthusiasm, thereby adding to your happiness.

_____

_____

_____

_____

_____

_____

92) Do a Mind Map of Everything That Is Happening in This Present Moment

This exercise cultivates mindfulness. Mindfulness is attending to NOW. Mind-map everything that is happening in the present moment, every detail you can grasp—the sounds, sights, feelings, etc. Being mindful calms you, stills your mind, like a pool of water in the forest. All kinds of strange and wonderful "animals" will come to drink at the pool, and you will clearly see the nature of things. Many strange and wonderful things will come and go, but you will remain still. This is happiness.

_____

_____

_____

_____

_____

_____

_____

93) Do a Mind Map for All the People You Wish to Send Loving-Kindness

Do a mind map for sending out loving-kindness to strangers, associates, friends, family, and yourself. Make those the branches, and from each branch, write what you wish for each. Examples:

May I accept this "unpleasant aspect" of the person.
May I be aware of this person's wish to be happy.
May I open to this person's suffering with acceptance, compassion, and kindness.
May this person be filled with loving-kindness.
May this person be well.
May this person be peaceful and at ease.
May this person be happy physically.
May this person be happy mentally.

As you go through this process, feel each phrase as vividly as possible. This is a powerful exercise because you are giving a precious gift to people. You are thinking of them in a positive way. You are trying to have a positive impact on their lives with nothing in return except the knowledge of your thoughts.

_____

_____

_____

_____

_____

_____

_____

_____

94) Visualizing Peace

Visualize walking through peaceful places and draw a map of images as you traverse from one place to another. Where do you end up? What can you incorporate from these places in your daily life?

Imagine a safe, protected, peaceful place—maybe somewhere in a forest or on a beach. Experience this place fully and with all your senses. Take as much time as you need.

Write down what you see and the sensations and images involved. At each branch of the mind map, allow yourself to rest in the feelings of comfort, safety, and tranquility this peaceful place evokes. Spend as much time in this place as you wish. Making peace within yourself is a much easier task than making world peace. But if each person in the world visualizes peace, then the world has a chance of experiencing peace, one person at a time. Listen to the messages. Keep the peace within yourself, and then you can bring peace to others.

Peace is a daily, a weekly, a monthly process, gradually changing opinions, slowly eroding old barriers, quietly building new structures.

—John F. Kennedy

_____

_____

_____

95) Doors

Open the door to your heart, from the inside. Mind-map an open door and then draw a path to other, labeled, doors you would like to open. Doors are symbolic for opening up your mind and heart to new thoughts and adventures. Maybe one is "make a new friend"; others might involve feelings you want to experience, a place you want to visit, a work goal you want to accomplish. You will never know what is on the other side unless you open the doors.

Do any of the doors lead to others? Are there connections? Take a few mindful breaths before you open each door. Each door can lead to a higher level of awareness. Plan to enter each door thoughtfully and reverently. Open these doors to experience independent contentment.

There are things that are known, and things that are un-known. In between there are doors.

                                 —William Blake

---

96) Conversations

Recall a conversation and write down what you remember as the main points. Map in the motivation or intention behind the things you said, and then note the response or effect of your speech.

It is important to pay attention, not just to *what* you say, but why, when, and how you say it. Even the thoughts behind speech are important. This exercise is something to practice to help you learn to consider each word carefully, so that what you say is "right" in form and content. By being in the present moment when you speak, you are more aware of what—and why, when, and how—you are saying it. You will have greater command of your speech, thus making what you say more meaningful.

Look at the state of mind that precedes what you say, the motivation for your comments and responses. Do this without judgment. Just note the motivation. Also note the effect of the speech. What kind of response did it get? Compassion or love? Irritation or silence?

This exercise helps you learn how to refrain from false or harmful speech, from gossip, slander, and silly nattering. Don't beat yourself up when you write things down and wonder why you said them. Use this as a learning tool for future conversations.

---

97) Improving Well-Being

Map out ways you can work for the well-being of people, animals, plants, and minerals. What can you do to better the world? Think-ing of others, helping others, any other ways of getting "outside" yourself—all of this makes you feel much happier. When you help others in need, you wake up to the fact that you do not have it so bad. When you look at it in a very broad scope, everyone and everything on this planet can potentially need your help.

There are even neuroscience studies indicating the positive ben-efits of getting out of ourselves. When we act generously toward oth-ers, our left prefrontal lobe of our neocortex gets activated, which stimulates feelings of happiness—and our bodies are flooded with feel-good hormones and our immune functions are boosted. So even science is telling us to find ways to improve the well-being of others on this planet.

Focus this mind map on others, on what *you* can do to make things better all around you. Living with the philosophy of making the Earth a better place than it was before you arrived is a sure bet for achieving a happier outlook on life.

---

98) Cleaning Out

Cleaning up the clutter, getting rid of trash, and donating unused items to those who could use them can bring much happiness. Map out all the places you need to clean out, both physical and mental. Draw receptacles where the trash goes. The project is not carried out to make room for more "stuff," but rather as a cleansing, detoxing, and simplification exercise. A key ingredient to living a happier life is simplifying it. When you see all the "stuff" that you are cleaning out, you will be amazed by how many things you purchased that you did not really need. Hopefully, it will be a first step toward simplifying your future.

Make it fun by categorizing the areas that you need to clean out. Draw cute trash containers. Maybe even put dates/deadlines for the various cleanup projects. If possible, be generous in donating items to worthy causes. Give things away that you will truly never use again (think clothes, books, old linens, dishes, and appliances), and take a moment to understand how much you are going to enrich someone else's life with your gift.

_____

_____

_____

_____

_____

_____

_____

99) Dealing with Anger

When you can, just before you show anger with your words, actions, or in writing, jot down what you are going to say and map out the possible consequences and reactions. This is especially helpful if you were going to write something—an e-mail or letter or memo—or were going to leave a voice-mail or text message. For the latter, pause for a few seconds or a minute and in your mind go over everything. Stopping/pausing the anger often lets you see that although you may enjoy that moment of blowing off steam, you don't gain anything in the long run.

Doing this mind map and then *letting go* is a better way of dealing with anger. Since very few people, even when confronted, admit they were wrong, then *not* confronting them relieves you of dealing with a situation that could cause you even more suffering or anger. This is a preventive exercise because now you will not have to expend the time and energy necessary to repair the damage that your anger would have caused.

100) Reading

As you read books that interest you, add Post-its and mind-map ideas, feelings, reactions to what you read. Really use your books and become part of them with Post-it notes or flags, penciled-in notes written in the margins, or a notebook devoted to your thoughts on reading.

You could use these in the future to trigger ideas, improve spelling skills, tackle new words, or expand your vocabulary. These notes can come in handy for brainstorming. Whether you are tackling a problem or trying to create something, others' ideas can provide a fresh perspective. As you age, your brain becomes filled with all kinds of information. It is impossible to store everything. By keeping notes of your readings, you solve two problems: First, by writing down information, you force yourself to understand it more at that moment. Second, you will have an accessible record of information that was important to you at the time, for easy reference or review. You can feel the happiness about to burst out!

_____

_____

_____

_____

_____

_____

_____

_____

101) Mapping a Thought Process

Map your thoughts, noting whether they are beneficial or harmful. Becoming more aware of your thought process can be very helpful to your ultimate goal: happiness. Understanding the process helps you see that you are not your thoughts; that you can give negative thoughts a chance to settle down, and even let them go; and instead, you can focus on positive, loving thoughts.

You may think that what goes on in your brain is not part of your karma, but it absolutely is. There is cause and effect with your thoughts as well as your speech and actions. Like your body, your mind needs training for optimal performance. By becoming more aware of your thought process, you are training yourself to have more control over your mind. When you have positive control of your mind, it can only have a positive effect on your happiness.

This exercise is informative and helps you cultivate the ability to allow a thought to slip by and not chase after it, remaining purely an observer.

---

102) The Unpleasant Stuff

Map the things you feel aversion to during the day, the things that you find unpleasant, try to avoid, or cause you suffering. Some are necessary feelings that are part of your job/career or family life. But some are unnecessary and can be avoided, with practice.

Feelings of aversion come and go. They are the mind's natural response to recognizing or recalling something unpleasant. Mind-map some that you become aware of today. Acknowledge them in this way and try to smile. As you write them down, let them go without getting caught up in them. Mapping them out helps you become conscious of how much negative time and energy you spend on them. By practicing how to let them go, you give yourself all kinds of extra time and energy to do the things that make you happy.

_____

_____

_____

_____

_____

_____

_____

PART 3: KEEPING A JOURNAL

Henry David Thoreau was one of the greatest thinkers and philosophers America has ever seen. One of his biggest influences, and great friend, was Ralph Waldo Emerson. Upon meeting Thoreau, Emerson suggested that he begin to keep a journal. Thoreau did so on an almost daily basis. Luckily for us, Thoreau took Emerson's advice. My advice to you is the same. This is my way of inspiring you to begin a journal that will help you lead a happier life.

103) Journal Entry of a Moment You Planned For, What Its Best-Case Scenario Was, and How It Actually Transpired

Take something like a wedding, birth, graduation, promotion, major birthday—and describe what you *wanted* it to be like. How long did you plan the event, including expectation in your thoughts? How much time was involved, and how long did the event actually last? Then, describe how it really played out. How much control did you actually have? If you had not had such high expectations, would things have been better? Would the results have been more satisfying? What can you learn from this about being in the present moment, doing some planning, but then just letting things "be"?

_____

_____

_____

_____

_____

_____

104) Drawing Your Journal Entry for the Day

If you know how to write, you already know how to draw. Some people are great writers but truly believe they have no drawing skills. It is in description that the keeper of a diary becomes an artist. All description is art, and in describing an event, action, or a being, you enter into the joy of art. But writing about things is only one way to document them. Sketching is another. No self-consciousness is allowed! Please draw your day on this page.

Drawing is also a form of meditation and makes you more aware, more alive in this present moment. By sitting quietly and drawing instead of being pulled inward to your old thoughts and desires, you can express wonderment in everything you experienced today. Drawing skills are not important in this exercise. Even if you make stick figures, that is okay. By taking the time to render the day on paper, you acknowledge the sacredness of each and every little thing.

_____

_____

_____

_____

_____

_____

_____

105) Journal Entry of a Mundane Task You Turned Into a Zen Moment or Meditation

Write about a mundane task or errand in detail, as if you were describing a major project. Be aware that each detail represents some precious moments of your time on Earth. Can you find the spiritual value in treating such a task as a meditation or "Zen moment"? Can you find a way to enjoy the struggle of completing mundane tasks? Even the simplest of tasks embodies the greatest spiritual happiness when performed calmly and with a quiet mind.

Focus on each part of what is done, all the while being mindful. Focus on just one thing at a time. Write about carrying this out with all of your being, not rushing. Make sure you are not thinking about all the other things you could be doing and accomplishing while you are working on this task. Appreciate the task(s) you have accomplished. The time you spend doing a task is precious. It is a time for being alive. When you practice mindful living, peace and happiness will bloom in your daily activities. Total absorption in a task is meditation.

----

106) "Finding the Bright Spots" Journal Entry

This exercise reminds you that every event and situation has a positive value. You have control over the menu of thoughts and images in your mind, and if you dwell on the positive ones, they will inspire you. You can spend a lifetime berating yourself for things that you have done or events that have happened to you—or, you can try to find the bright spots in these experiences and turn them into affirmations. Realizing that we have the ability to make a choice on these matters is a key to happiness.

Verbalize the positive. Pick a recent event or situation that you perceive as negative; then, look for the good in it. The trick is to see every situation from both a realistic and an upbeat viewpoint, at the same time. How did you deal with the difficult situation? Did you suffer from your own response to it? What could/should you let go of? What has to be accepted? What lesson might be learned from the difficulty? What hidden value or positive element can you glean from this event? Your prospects will brighten with an influx of optimistic thoughts. By undergoing a difficult situation with grace, you are creating good karma. There are positive benefits and spiritual lessons that troubles can provide. When you talk or communicate with other people, look to see if and how they find the bright spot when they tell you stories about themselves. When someone else looks for the bright spots in their lives, you can also benefit from that affirmative power.

_____

_____

_____

_____

_____

_____

_____

107) Art Journal Entry of Happy Stuff

Spontaneous, unedited, fresh, and bold (in color!)—this is you, taking an art journey into your head, your heart, your dreams. Use this entry to discover the many ways that you are art! It is about transferring your spirit to the surface—whatever part of your vast essence that you can draw on at any creative moment. Anyone can make an artistic visual journal, and it can take any form you choose.

Your journal entry does not have to be cute or happy or provocative, and you do not need fancy materials. Embark on a mini journey, capturing your feelings, even if you think you lack artistic skills or don't have the time. Drop any fears that may block your creative expression. Create a fun manifesto that is YOU by letting the hidden artist in you come out.

_____

_____

_____

_____

_____

_____

_____

108) Journal Entry of Words Found in Magazines That Describe Happiness in a Personal Way for You

Get your hands on some magazines and cut out pictures and words that mean "happiness" to you. Create an art journal entry to reflect your personal approach.

Add to this art journal with more words and pictures, or more pages over time. Take the time to reflect on the types of pictures and words you have chosen. Why did you choose the pictures and words that you did? Do these things exist in your life right now? Are they things/feelings you want? Can you art-journal some of the steps you need to take to achieve more happiness?

_____

_____

_____

_____

_____

_____

109) Describing Your Favorite Songs and How They Make You Feel

Music stirs powerful emotions in all of us. In the age of iPods, you may have your favorite songs all together on a little machine—even categorized. Or, you may be from the generation that remembers buying

LPs and 45s and cassette tapes at your favorite music store. Did you have a favorite radio station or DJ that you listened to at home or while cruising in the car? Have you thought about how these songs make you feel—how these songs define feelings that you have/had? How you felt when you realized that you are not the only person in the world to feel that way? When you haven't heard a favorite song in a while and you listen to it, what happens to your mood?

Choose ten favorite songs and describe how they make you feel, and why you think they have the effect they do. Are there events or people connected to those songs? Were you of a certain age? Are they mainly positive/happy songs, or is there another theme?

"Layla" (Derek & the Dominos)

"Lola" (The Kinks)

"In My Life" (The Beatles)

"Up on the Roof" (James Taylor)

"Send in the Clowns" (Judy Collins)

"If You Love Somebody, Set
  Them Free" (Sting)

"If I Loved You" (from the
  musical *Carousel*)

"Pink Houses" (John
  Mellencamp)

"Marrakesh Express"
  (Crosby, Stills &
  Nash)

_____

_____

_____

_____

110) Epicurus and Happiness

When we say that pleasure is the end, we do not mean the pleasure of the profligate or that which depends on physical enjoyment—as some think who do not understand our teachings, disagree with them, or give them an evil interpretation—but by pleasure we mean the state wherein the body is free from pain and the mind from anxiety.
—Epicurus, Greek philosopher (342–270 BC)

Write about Epicurus's statement that we should occupy our time with things which make us happy, because happiness makes our lives complete and is the goal of all our actions. Do you think this is a selfish approach to life?

Happiness for Epicurus is a "natural condition" we are born with, something we can get back. It is neither too early nor too late to seek happiness; it can be a constant feature of life and it can endure throughout even the most painful circumstances. Do you, like Epicurus, agree that pleasure is the primary and innate good? Is it fine to make it our "starting point" in deciding what to do and what not to do? Do we come back to it every time we want to assess the goodness of anything? Epicurus believed it was okay to do happy things as long as they did not negatively affect other people—something to consider.

_____

_____

_____

_____

_____

_____

111) Deep, Heartfelt Happiness

Write about the times when you felt deep, heartfelt happiness, and what you were doing then; how could you re-create that experience now? These memories will not be difficult to recall because you have probably given them some thought already. However, this exercise takes you a step further because you are doing more than just thinking about the happiness—you are writing it down.

Describe what may have led up to this experience of deep, heartfelt happiness. Put the actual event into words. Also, describe how long this feeling lasted, or how long you have remembered this vividly.

Were there things you did that led to this feeling of joy, which you could do again? Was there a clear cause and effect, or did this emotion seem to arrive by chance? Were other people involved? Were you at a specific place? Were you at a certain age?

By remembering and recording these experiences, you will not only relive past happiness, but also open your heart for more in the future.

_____

_____

_____

_____

_____

_____

_____

112) No Thanks

Write up what you are *not* seeking, that which you will not suffer, and what will not bring the happiness you seek.

This book has focused on the positive, but part of knowing what brings you happiness is also being aware of what you do not want or do not feel you can handle. This is the other side of the coin.

Don't make a long, whiny list. Stick to the major points, your major aversions or dislikes. After you write them down, describe whether or not you believe you have control over these things.

- I don't want to go on a diet (although I *would* like to lose weight).
- I don't want to buy lots of stuff to keep up with the Joneses.
- I don't want to be needy or greedy or stupid when I reach old age.
- I don't want to succumb to all sorts of medical treatments, but would rather let nature take its course.
- I don't want to "retire."

_____

_____

_____

_____

_____

_____

_____

113) Nothingness

An unused diary can bring as much pleasure as a filled one, just from staring at the blank pages.

_____

_____

_____

_____

_____

_____

_____

_____

114) TV

Write a journal entry describing what television shows have drawn you over the past few years. What do the themes of these shows mean when analyzed in relation to your life? Is the television mainly used as an escape, or as a learning opportunity?

Are you drawn to shows about the type of person you would like to be? Are you drawn to watching people of a certain age range? Do the programs deal with moral issues? Do the channels you watch have commercials, or are they commercial-free? Is there a fascination with certain genres—comedy or medical drama, reality TV, or sports or talk shows? What do you think your choices say about you? Are you wasting your time? Do you usually watch your shows alone or with other people? Do you usually eat any meals or snacks while watching certain shows? If you watch certain shows with another person or other people, is it usually quiet, or is there a lot of chatter? Could the time spent watching television be more selective, or be eliminated or cut back?

_____

_____

_____

_____

_____

_____

115) Busyness

Write about how happy you are when you are busy, especially in your free time. When you are busy in your free time and happy about it, does it apply to clear goals you have set for yourself? Does happiness involve knowing how well you are doing during the activity, even if the feedback is just from yourself? When you are busy and happy, are you usually alone or with another person or other people? Is the activity more physical or mental in nature?

During happy, nonwork activities, do you feel that you are balancing the skills you bring to the activities with the challenges they present? Does the time spent also merge actions with awareness? How well do you avoid distractions? Can you forget yourself, the time, even your surroundings? This is called _flow_.

What is the relationship between flow and happiness? Do you sense happiness when you are in the middle of flow? Probably not; this usually occurs afterwards. And the more flow you experience in daily life, the more likely you are to feel happy overall, especially if you have flow in work as well as nonwork activities.

_____

_____

_____

_____

_____

_____

_____

116) Happiness Diary

Keep a happiness diary to record your good moments in detail, with feeling.

Every day, promise yourself a few minutes to write three thoughtful, detailed things down. Everybody, yes, everybody, can find three of those each day. If you wrote three happy thoughts a day, you would end up with 1,095 happy thoughts in your diary over the course of a year. Maybe it is something you read or heard or saw. Do not censor and do not worry about duplicating an earlier entry. It is a happiness diary, and you cannot will it to be a certain way any more than you could will a traditional diary to record a day other than how it actually transpired. Remember to periodically read what you wrote for added happiness.

_____

_____

_____

_____

_____

_____

117) Daily Progress

Create journal entries of your daily progress to finding more happiness to reinforce positive traits, maintain your enthusiasm, and bring you closer to your goals. By concentrating on the daily progress, you build up a sound foundation for long-term happiness. It all begins in the short term by becoming aware of your daily progress.

It can be a personal progress report, a pat on the back that will keep you inspired. You need to reinforce each day how much of your happiness is up to you. You cannot rely on other people to consistently recognize the progress that you make. They do not control your happiness; it comes from within. When you recognize the progress you're making, it just keeps on building, and comes to mean something quite special. Be generous to yourself, but don't try to fool yourself. The way you see—and feel about—yourself affects what you believe to be true about yourself.

_____

_____

_____

_____

_____

_____

_____

118) Love Letters

Today, write a love letter straight from the heart to the person you feel the most for—whether they've passed away or are still living. Great understanding comes with great love. Become aware of what love means to you. This unconditional love can be described in any way you want. Visualize the person and allow your feelings of love to rise up. Imagine you are embracing and protecting them with this love. There are many different types of love you can feel, so don't limit it just to a spouse or significant other. Expand it to children, relatives, and friends.

Write about what you most love and appreciate about this person. Describe how you love this person, and, if they are still living, how you would like to show more love with words, actions, touch, thoughtful-

ness. Even add a poem if you like. You are writing this without expecting any-thing in return. This exercise is not about trying to understand how this person feels (or felt) about you; it's about your personal feelings. You are practicing the art of offering overflow-ing love and seeking nothing in return.

_____

_____

_____

_____

_____

_____

119) Spiritual Quotes

You must live in the present, launch yourself on every wave, find your eternity in each moment.

—Henry David Thoreau

Pick a quotation from your favorite spiritual book or a spiritual quote from a quotations resource. Write about what you think it means and what lesson you can take from it. It is always a great surprise when someone can express exactly how you feel or think in an elegant and truthful way. The meaning that can come out of only a few sentences can be truly inspiring and life-changing.

> *If one advances confidently in the direction of one's dreams, and endeavors to live the life which one has imagined, one will meet with a success unexpected in common hours.*
>
> —Henry David Thoreau

Is this quote particularly meaningful to you right now, or has it been special to you for a while? Is it something you strive to attain or maintain? Is there a theme to the quotes that you choose? Do you select quotes from one particular person, a few people, or many people? Quotes can act as reminders of wise thoughts and guiding precepts for living a happy life.

_____

_____

_____

_____

_____

_____

_____

120) Precious Moments

Recall precious moments in your day that made a difference to you and write about them. As you go through the day, register when you are happy and take note of the precipitating event or circumstance.

You will become aware of moments that positively affect you. This creates a log of memories that will make you feel good. By constantly asking yourself about your current state of happiness, you are putting yourself in the driver's seat and making an important first step in taking responsibility for your overall happiness. You will also discover what types of moments make you feel happy. Are they big things or small things? Do they involve other people, or are you alone? Are you at a particular place, or is it a specific time? It is helpful to analyze the occurrences of precious moments in your life.

_____

_____

_____

_____

_____

_____

121) Heroes

Write about an extraordinary person who is your hero. What is it about the person that makes you feel this way—do they have certain qualities, like selflessness, courage, and determination in the face of adversity? Or is it their achievements in life; their job, looks, or possessions; their partner, or lifestyle? Have you learned anything from this person that you have been able to translate to your own life? How do you define the word *hero*? Do you know them personally, or just about them? Knowing that all heroes are human, how would you feel if your hero fell from their perch? Has this already happened to you? As a society, do we need heroes?

Would you like to have the fearless attitude of a hero? Do you think you are a hero to anyone? Is it important to you to become a hero to someone? What would you say about the following quotation:

> *When we quit thinking primarily about ourselves and our own self-preservation, we undergo a truly heroic transformation of consciousness.*
>
> —Joseph Campbell

Maybe you could become a hero to yourself; would you consider that a great achievement?

_____

_____

_____

_____

_____

_____

_____

122) What Makes You Laugh?

Write a journal entry about things that make you laugh. Do you laugh when something silly goes wrong, or when you get caught up in something small? Do you laugh at human foibles, at jokes, at mistakes, at stories, at life? Do

you ever laugh at the expense of other people? Do you laugh a little — or often? Do you wish you could laugh more? Describe how you feel physically after a laugh attack, and how you feel when you hear someone else laughing.

Every morning upon waking, before opening your eyes, stretch like a cat. After a few minutes, with your eyes still closed, begin to laugh. For up to five minutes, just laugh. At first, you will be forcing it, but then genuine laughter will come. It may take a few days to get used to this. Before long, it will become spontaneous and will change the whole nature of your day.

----

123) Poetry

First, start by reading some poetry. Try to connect with some poems that are new to you or reconnect with ones that were important to you in the past.

Then, write about a poem that moves you. Poems have the ability to inspire us in many ways. When you find a poem that is pleasing to you, no matter its length, you enjoy it because the author has triggered something inside of you that hits home. That is the magic of poetry. That is what this exercise is trying to accomplish.

Next, write your own poem for yourself or for someone else. To jump-start this journal entry, open a poetry book or look at a poetry website and pick a line, any line, from a poem. Just pick something that jumps out at you. Make that the first line of your poem.

Another method of starting your poem is to open a thesaurus and grab a word; you can either start with it, or write your whole poem about that word.

Did you write any poems as a child? See if you can find one. If you do, change it to fit yourself now. Writing poetry is a very personal experience because you are thinking deeply about what you are trying to write. Poems by their very nature are succinct; you need to measure your words and keep it brief, thereby getting to the heart of the matter. You are aware of feelings, experiences, and things.

Share the poem with someone else, or even write one for them.

_____

_____

_____

_____

_____

_____

_____

_____

124) Newness

Write about your appreciation for new things: new people, experiences, and ideas. Each moment is a new life. It is change. Newness has a way of offering us hope. With awareness, you can see this. Each moment is a fresh start, open to new opportunities, new personal growth. This journal entry treats everything as new—because in each moment, everything *is* new and changed. This is about enjoying that newness, the surprises. Look at everything as if for the first time. Write about your appreciation for the newness, the change, having a life like this.

Beginnings are brand-new chances.
Every day, look up one new word in a dictionary.
There is always a new way to say something old.
Learn something new each day.
New life is everywhere you look.

_____

_____

_____

_____

_____

_____

_____

125) Nice Things to Say

Keep a list in your journal of nice things you could say to a particular person or persons. This is especially helpful to try with someone you do not like, but have to deal with. If you are completing this exercise about someone you have issues with, let the problem be theirs. Let them spend time and suffer the consequences of negative thoughts and feelings. By training yourself to say nice things, you have the ability to set the tone when you do meet up with this person. You also never have to worry about someone coming back to you and asking why you said something unpleasant about them.

Is what you want to say an improvement on silence? It is best to hold it all in until you have figured out how to say something in a useful way. It is always better to say something kind or encouraging. Saying positive things may even have the other person questioning and reevaluating their own feelings. Apply meditation in action to ensure that what you say is pleasant. Your list of nice things to say will help you with this.

- That is a great color on you.
- I hope you are well and happy.
- I like your hair in that style.
- You seem to be having a good day.
- How is your work going?

Keep track of the reactions you get when you employ these nice things to say. You will be pleasantly surprised to find that even if you do not like someone, you can still have a positive relationship with them.

_____

_____

_____

_____

_____

_____

_____

126) Blog

If you are interested in sharing a bit of your life with others, look into creating an Internet journal or blog, a phenomenon that has taken hold in recent years. It seems that people really have a lot to say these days, and want to make their opinions known. Are you one of them? Would you like to be? Have you participated on others' sites, but haven't yet started your own?

If you are really into journaling, there are thousands of Internet sites devoted to this practice, and some are designed solely by online journals. You give up a certain amount of privacy when keeping an online journal, but maybe you feel like sharing a portion (or all) of your life with others. There is potential here for gaining a better understanding of each other, as well as ourselves.

127) A Philosophy to Live By

Throughout history, some of the greatest thinkers on this planet have attempted to form meaningful life philosophies. Trying to answer the big questions in life is no trivial pursuit. Use your journal to help you formulate a philosophy to live by. Purpose is what brings meaning to your life, and the recognition that you are part of a larger whole. Philosophy attempts to clarify your thoughts and answer the big question, "Why am I here?" You have to be able to wonder in order to develop a philosophy. Whether you just scratch the surface of philosophical thought or dig deep inside of it, if you have a clear philosophy of life and a defined sense of purpose, you are likely to be happy and successful. When you lack purpose, you may feel aimless, dissatisfied, or restless.

Some lucky people have always known what they want out of life. Are you one of them? Do you know that you can have happiness anytime, anyplace, anywhere, no matter the external circumstances? Take the time to sit down and contemplate your sense of purpose, your basic philosophy of life. Maybe doing your best is the only philosophy you will ever need, but you must follow through with action. Let your personal philosophy inspire you with courage.

128) If

If you could do anything in the world right now, what would it be? Answer this question, ignoring cost, skill, or anything that might hold you back from achieving this goal.

What do you dream about doing that you have never done? Would achieving this objective help fulfill your philosophy or purpose in life? Would it give you the feeling that you had done something really worthwhile? If the answer to at least one of these questions is yes, then you truly must pursue this somehow—investigate what you can do to bring it into reality. If you can imagine something, then it is possible.

While completing this exercise, look at any common themes that become obvious in your "ifs." Are most of your "ifs" about helping people? Or, are most of them about doing something adventurous? Or about changing a career or job? In your quest to become more aware of yourself, this exercise will challenge you to find the "ifs" that will help you achieve greater happiness.

_____

_____

_____

_____

_____

_____

_____

129) Writing

Whatever you have been holding back from writing—poetry, fiction, a play, essays, etc.—just start. Writing and art are very similar, in that

we have so much fear that we often find we "cannot do" these creative endeavors. The problem lies in the judgment, including prejudgment, that we bring to the table. Who can really say that any writing or art is "good" or "bad"? That is judgment. And guess what? You can choose to let go of judgment, especially with your own art and writing. As with most skills in life, the only way to improve them is through practice, practice, and more practice. The more you write, the more proficient you will become.

Now, start writing what you have always wanted to write. There is nothing wrong with starting off slowly and building on your success. Writing a little each day adds up to a lot in a short time. Do you have poems inside you? A play? A television show pilot? Essays? A novel? Who says that the only (or immediate) goal is publication or payment? *Write!* Say to yourself only, "In this lifetime, I would like to get this out to the public"—or "I will leave this to my children to publish." Then have fun with your new project.

_____

_____

_____

_____

_____

_____

_____

_____

130) History

Become a historian. Decide which aspects of the past are compelling and pursue them, focusing on the sources and details that are personally meaningful, recording findings in your personal style.

Maybe you want to compile a history of your family. Maybe you want to study old maps and compare them. Or you might be interested in the history of your home—the evolution of its structure, or the name of its previous owners. What about your town's history?

Is there a time period that fascinates you? Do you suspect you may have lived in that time period during a previous life? Make history your teacher. Learning from history may eliminate mistakes in the future or initiate some creative thinking.

_____

_____

_____

_____

_____

_____

_____

_____

131) Be an Amateur Philosopher

Become an amateur philosopher, writing down the basic questions that interest you, and what past thinkers have said about them. Read, talk, and then write about these ideas. Try to sketch out answers that will help make sense of your own experiences.

First, make a list of your questions. Research what other philosophers have said about these questions. Then, talk to others about the questions and use keywords in online searches to see what else is out there that may be applicable or useful in formulating your own answers.

_____

_____

_____

_____

_____

_____

_____

_____

132) Happiness, the By-Product

Write an entry about the fact that happiness is always a by-product, not the result of a direct pursuit. Happiness happens when you are not thinking about it.

Write about the following:

- Happiness is a by-product of a thoughtful, disciplined life.
- Happiness is a by-product of an effort to make someone else happy.
- "Happiness is not something that can be demanded from life.

Virtue is simple happiness, and happiness is a by-product of function. You are happy when you are functioning." —William S. Burroughs

- "Happiness is mostly a by-product of doing what makes us feel fulfilled." —Benjamin Spock

_____

_____

_____

_____

_____

_____

_____

133) Courage

Write a few paragraphs about "If I had the courage to do it, I would . . ."

Author Scott Turow wrote, "Courage is not the absence of fear but the ability to carry on with dignity in spite of it." And happiness really is a form of courage. All our dreams can come true if we just have the courage to pursue them.

By writing about something you have been afraid to do, you are asking for the grace to realize who you are and the courage you need to do this. Courage also exists in the success of something. When you succeed at doing something, it may mean your whole life is going to change. You have to prepare yourself for that, too.

_____

_____

_____

_____

_____

_____

_____

134) Afterlife

Give it some thought and construct for yourself an afterlife you can believe in. See if these convictions give you strength.

What are your beliefs concerning the time after death? Are you afraid of death? Why? Does that fear have to do with the unknown aspects of the afterlife? What type of afterlife would cause you to feel no fear? Would reincarnation/rebirth be better? Knowing you had a chance to come back and start over—would you fear or welcome that? Where do you believe you will go after death? Like Woody Allen said, "There is a fear that there is an afterlife but no one will know where it's being held."

_____

_____

_____

_____

_____

_____

_____

_____

135) Writing on the Go

Keep a journal in your car and/or a small one in your purse or brief-case so that when you feel like writing, you won't have to wait.

It is better to write when things come to you—at appropriate times, of course. When you write something down as soon as it occurs to you, your writing will capture the meaning of your thought more accurately than if you wrote it down later. You don't want to stop meditating to write down an idea, and you should not write while you are driving. But when you stop—when the bell gongs, when the car is parked, when you are waiting in a line—those are great times to write journal entries, lists, and mind maps.

_____

_____

_____

_____

_____

_____

_____

136) Intimacy

Keep a journal entry to chronicle your path to greater intimacy by writing down the things you should say to or do for others.

The skills of intimacy do not come easily for many of us. We complain about the lack of intimacy in our lives, yet we do little ourselves to foster it. "Being yourself" is basically the idea, but with good intentions and careful speech. By occasionally sharing how you feel and what you are thinking, you can deepen your relationships with family and friends.

Be mindful of your need for intimacy, as well as the needs of others. Trust in the difficult. Communication is a continual balancing act, juggling the conflicting needs for intimacy and independence. What can you do for (or say to) others to create more intimacy? Is being a great listener the best thing you can offer them?

137) Jealousy

Write about someone you are jealous of, about what you think they have that you don't. Then write about why this is so, and what you can do about it—or whether you should do anything at all. Jealousy is an issue we all have to deal with. The person or people you are jealous of have no control over the fact you are jealous of them. They

are totally innocent, and you have to realize that it's your issue to sort out.

This journal exercise is designed to
help you "un-learn" jealousy. Jealousy
indicates that you don't like something about yourself. It may seem to
be directed toward others, but in truth,
your jealousies point back to you, and
what you believe are your own shortcom-
ings, weaknesses, faults, and disappointments.
Jealousy is also connected with fear—you're afraid
of losing something you possess. Jealousy is not envy or love of another, but rather reveals a focus on self-love, which corrodes the heart
and actually makes you feel ugly.

To cure jealousy is to see it for what it is: dissatisfaction with self.
The self is something you can have control over, and this journal exercise should help you gain that control.

_____

_____

_____

_____

_____

_____

_____

_____

138) Now

Write about where you are now in your life. What events mark it off:
spouse, kids, parents, school, career? How far back does this period reach? What have been the main characteristics of this recent

period? Enter memories and facts in this journal entry, without judgment or censorship.

After you have determined what NOW is to you, decide whether or not you like NOW. Would you prefer a drastic change? Do you see a major change happening soon, like school, marriage, child, a career change, or retirement? If your NOW is not what you had hoped it would be, do you feel that you have the power and courage to change it? Do you feel that you have to stick it out in your NOW for a while? If you enjoy your NOW, how can you maintain it? Where are you? Are you here—in NOW? Maybe you have been elsewhere. This exercise exists totally in describing NOW.

\
\
\
\
\
\
\
\

139) Dialogue

Choose a person to "talk" with in your mind and write out dialogues about topics that are important to you, in ways that this person might help or guide you. You can do the same with dialogues with your body, with work, with society, and with events.

This journal exercise deals with the connective relationships within your life. It is part of the realm of interior communication, and how all of its mini-processes work to distract and confuse us. We start out in life perfect, a seed of possibility. Then our minds develop all kinds of ways to move us from this calm, empty center that we began with.

Writing out such dialogues can help empty the mind. We seek our true spiritual nature and a quiet mind by emptying our thoughts onto paper.

140) I Remember

Begin with "I remember," and write down lots of small memories. Don't be concerned with when the event happened, or try to keep them in any specific order, or whether they were good or bad. Go for names, places, events, etc. Include as much detail as you can.

When you are finished, evaluate the tone of the memories. This is where you really have to look at what you wrote. Look for obvious themes. Are they mainly happy, or sad? This is a stream-of-consciousness journal entry. The brain calls on good memories in order to experience good feelings. In order to increase happiness, you have to train your mind to go to the good places as it reaches into the memory bank. Even if you are under the impression that your past was not that happy, try to recall as many positive things as you can. Reliving these experiences will bring good feelings from the past into the present. This is a happiness skill that is within your ability to accomplish, and one you can use over and over.

_____

_____

_____

_____

_____

_____

_____

_____

141) A Place You Love

Visualize and write about a place that you really love, whether it is real or fantasy. Be there. See the details. Write the details.

Paying attention to the little things is important for happiness. It is easy to be happy in a place you love. The difficult part is trying to find happiness in bad situations. Sometimes everything seems to be against us. It is during these times that this exercise will help us achieve happiness. Even when you are in a bad situation, you can look around and find something small that is good.

This journal exercise trains you to notice details in a happy place. After practicing with the places you love, the training will come to your aid when you really need it. The same way you notice details in a happy place, you will try to find happy details in a bad situation. Visit this place in your journal for comfort and healing.

142) Closeness to Nature

Answer the following question in your journal: What is the closest you have ever felt to nature? Write about that. Feel the experience again as you write about it.

Time spent in nature is healing, from feeling the warmth of the sand at the beach to seeing your breath on a cold winter day. Write about your closeness to nature. Write about the physical and mental changes you experience when you are outdoors. Spend time enjoying nature as often as you can, as it can ground you and reaffirm your connection with the world. Pay attention to all the manifestations of the outside world. Have faith in nature. Align with nature. Let nature enhance your happiness. As Ralph Waldo Emerson said: "Nature is thoroughly mediate. It is made to serve . . . It offers all its kingdoms to man as the raw material which he may mould into what is useful."

_____

_____

_____

_____

_____

_____

_____

_____

_____

143) Time Slices

When your level of communication with a family member has changed, as with a son who has gone off to college, you can both write journals and then exchange them at the end of the year. You can chronicle your daily lives, your loves, hopes, fears, and frustrations, throughout the year. You can impart wisdom, anecdotes, and any advice that is appropriate.

Then, on January 1 of each new year, you can exchange the journals and each receive new, blank ones to start the process anew. The journals may be heartrending at times, as you are allowed inside the most intimate and fierce struggles of each other's lives. These journals can become priceless time slices.

_____

_____

_____

_____

_____

_____

_____

_____

_____

_____

144) Write All Day

Once a month, or quarter, or year, write all day in your journal, without talking to anybody. Choose a place where you will not be disturbed except for eating and sleeping. You will feel like you are on a roller coaster, both physically and mentally.

Yes, it is a meditation of sorts. Whereas meditation usually focuses on quiet, this one focuses on words—but with the same ultimate goal.

This one day will be focused on writing whatever you choose. Maintain silence, except on paper. Is this a difficult exercise for you to do? After completing this exercise, you will have gained an awful lot of knowledge about yourself.

_____

_____

_____

_____

_____

_____

145) Intriguing Happy Words

Make a list of words that intrigue you and also make you happy. Write a journal entry using all of these words.

The words can be used in a prose composition, or you can turn them into some type of poetry. Be creative. By intriguing, we mean that these are words you are drawn to for some reason, maybe ones you have been curious about and need to look up. Maybe the word elicits an emotion or feeling. You could use a thesaurus to compile the list of words you will use.

_____

_____

_____

_____

_____

_____

_____

146) The Only Thing I Ever Wanted

Think ten years ahead and write about this: "The only thing I ever wanted was . . ."

Maybe you are fifty years old. Imagine you are sixty, not fifty. The idea is to try to predict what will make you happy that far in the future. You may be surprised at some of the things you come up with. Dreams often enable us to fulfill our purpose in life.

Do you see how you could start working on this now? What are you waiting for? Ten years go by quickly. You can begin working on your happiness right now.

147) The Best Stuff in Life Is Free

Write about how the best stuff in life is free. If something is not free, then there is a cost to it. Understand the cost of things. Sometimes you pay more than money for them. But when something is free, you eliminate that cost and can enjoy the thing or event for what it is. What things—physical or mental—have you noticed and collected and used over the years that were free? Taking a walk is free, and can produce a tremendously positive physical feeling. Have you seen how this adage is especially true for young children? How many times have you seen children playing with the cardboard box the toy came in, instead of the toy?

Yearning for nothing can set you free to enjoy what you do, to really *see* things, to hear the music in all things. With the absence of always grasping for something more, you will be free, too.

_____

_____

_____

_____

_____

_____

_____

148) One-Liners

Jot down one-liners of philosophy, absurdity, or spiritual revelation that wander through your mind. Your collection can be words of wisdom that occur to you and to which you can refer in the future. Surprise yourself with the revelations.

Observations by other writers are wonderful to read and refer to, but do not discount your own understanding. Think of what you write as affirmations or guides to personal happiness and peace.

149) Fantasy

Record a fantasy in your journal. Close your eyes and think about what it would be like if your job, relationship, children, or (fill-in-the-blank) was perfect. Then write about your inner journey. Remember, it is a fantasy. Perfection cannot be achieved in reality. Don't let yourself get caught up in the fantasy. It is a tool to make your current place in life happier. What can you take from your fantasy and use in your life to make you happier, right now?

_____

_____

_____

_____

_____

_____

_____

_____

_____

150) Journal Lists

Create journal lists for clarifying thoughts, identifying patterns or problems, brainstorming solutions, getting below the surface, getting past the obvious, gathering a lot of information quickly, focusing attention on what is really going on. Writing down journal lists is a way to help you concentrate on the situation at hand. Whether problem-solving or being creative, the focus you experience by writing will help you. If you do this exercise in your mind, you may spend a lot of time repeating information. By writing it down, you will not repeat information and you will think of new—and more—things. When the mind is focused on something, it can work miracles.

_____

_____

_____

_____

_____

_____

_____

_____

_____

_____

_____

151) Meditate, then Write

Meditate for twenty to thirty minutes. The simplest formal meditation method is watching the breath. Sit comfortably, whatever that is for you. Let your eyes close gently. Invite your body to relax, and release into the ground or cushion. Become sensitive to and listen to your breath. Breathe through your nose. Feel the air as it goes in and out of the nostrils. Feel the rising and falling of the chest and abdomen.

Allow your attention to settle where you feel the breath most clearly. Focus there. Follow the breath. Allow the breath to be as it is without controlling it. Thinking will start. It is a habit. See each thought like a railroad car of a train going by. See it, acknowledge it, let it go, and come back to the breath. It does not matter how many times you get caught up in a thought, or for how long. Begin again and bring awareness back to the breath. If a physical sensation or pain arises, do the same. See it, acknowledge it without getting caught up in it, let it go, and come back to the breath. For twenty minutes, follow your breath with close attention. When your mind wanders, stop and come back to the breath.

Write about how you felt before, during, and now, after the meditation. Are there differences in how you feel, mentally and physically? Are there differences in what your thoughts contain? Do you feel it was beneficial to meditate?

Recording your meditation experiences gets you into the habit of both carrying out the process and analyzing its effects. You may be surprised to learn that the changes are subtle, sometimes too subtle to detect and describe. That does not mean that the benefits are not huge. Like anything worthwhile, practice—day after day—is the key.

_____

_____

_____

_____

_____

_____

_____

_____

_____

_____

152) 100-Year-Old Self

Have a conversation with your 100-year-old self. Take a deep breath and close your eyes. Imagine yourself at the ripe old age of 100, in perfect health, full of the wisdom of life experience. You are happy.

In this journal entry, have a conversation with this wise, wonderful person, asking what you should know, what you should concentrate on, what you should make your priorities in life. Ask what things you could do or experience that would have the most positive impact on your life.

Allow the answers to appear on the page. Don't edit yourself; let whatever thoughts come into your mind to flow into your journal, no matter how silly some may seem. There are no rules. Just write!

_____

_____

_____

_____

_____

_____

_____

_____

_____

153) What You Really Want

Write about the topic, "Is this what I really want?" Write the question in your own hand, then close your eyes and take three deep breaths. Now write for ten minutes about all the wonderful things you have in your life. Write about all the things you may have forgotten you wanted. Write about the things you let go of because they seemed too difficult or too time-sensitive or financially impossible. Let yourself write what you really, really want. Don't edit anything; just allow your thoughts to flow onto the page.

This is not the time to critique your dreams but instead, to simply get your desires down on the page. No one ever has to read this. Whatever the critic inside your head is saying to you, release it and surrender it. Keep writing your deepest dreams and desires, and soon the critical voice will fade into the background. As you write your dreams, you give them wings. They float off the page and conspire with the universe to bring you the life you really want. When you truly and honestly evaluate "what you really want," you will discover things on your list that are really not that important to you. Those are the items you want to fly away so you won't spend time and energy trying to go after them. The items that remain are where your time and energy should go. Who knows—with the extra time and energy, you may be able to achieve the things you really want.

_____

_____

_____

_____

_____

_____

_____

_____

154) Gratitude

Keep a journal on your nightstand. Each night before nodding off, write the numbers 1 through 5 on the page, and then fill in the blanks with things you are grateful for. You will begin to look for things throughout your day to write down each night. This practice shifts your focus away from what is  wrong in your life to what is right and beautiful and kind in the world. This exercise is a self-fulfilling one. When you begin to think about the things you are grateful for, you become more grateful for them. As you focus on both big and small things to be thankful for, soon, your world is filled with gratifying thoughts and experiences.

Another way to do this is to keep a gratitude journal in the kitchen and jot down a few things as you sip your first cup of coffee or tea in the morning. This is a lovely ritual for beginning your day on a positive note. If you set your alarm ten minutes earlier to do this exercise, you will have a better day.

Once you get going, gratitude will overflow from your journal because there are always so many things to be grateful for—and therein lies the magic. Expressing gratitude connects you to a state of appreciation that spills over into everything you do and experience.

_____

_____

_____

_____

_____

_____

155) Two-Line Journal

Creating a two-line journal offers you a way to focus on a single thought every day and to record it for later use. You have an entire day to come up with something that is important to you and break it down into two lines. Here is a list of ideas:

brilliant ideas you'd otherwise forget
short quotes and observations
thumbnail sketches of anything you like
happenings of the day
meaningful personal philosophies
a short rhyme
a grumble about the state of the world
a crisp, descriptive phrase or two about people, places, events, feelings, etc.

While it takes just a few minutes to write your thought, you search all day long for that one thing that deserves saving in your journal. Never create the two lines because you have to; write them down because they are important to you. They help define you as a person. This is not a trivial exercise. Knowing you need a line or two a day keeps you creatively aware, observant.

156) What You Would Do for a Living If You Thought You Could and You Had the Education to Do It

Perhaps this is a variation on the theme of "What is your dream job?" — but the question is more about whether you have the personality for your dream job. This makes the exercise more realistic because you truly have to consider whether or not you have the patience to be a chef or the people skills to be a personal organizer or the desire to work with children/teenagers as a teacher. Examining what you are best at, what you excel in—in relation to what you consider to be a fun and fulfilling work life—may be very useful. You could use this information to make a major education and/or career decision. Or you could use this evaluation to select a part-time pursuit (paid or otherwise) where you could "test the waters" and find out if you can indeed orchestrate a more ideal work life.

This is also an important exercise to complete if you are near retirement or retired. Retirement can offer people an incredible opportunity to pursue employment dreams. When you know yourself a little better, it helps in your pursuit.

---

157) Words of Happiness

With all the talk about pressure, tension, stress, unhappiness, et cetera—one would think that a good part of our vocabulary is negative. Surprisingly, a lot of our vocabulary is positive, optimistic, even happy. We have thousands of words to express positive emotions, things, states, conditions, actions, and qualities. It is truly interesting to look at optimistic, constructive, helpful, encouraging, affirmative, and upbeat words as a subset of our great English language. Choose ten words that are "happy" and write your own definition of each. Then write an example sentence for each, involving yourself or offering a quotation, etc. So look for happiness in the words you love.

advantage *n* something that puts you in a better position than others

> Little advantages . . . occur every day.
> —*Benjamin Franklin*

beautify *v* to make something more beautiful

> The gem of my life, the rose without thorns, who beautifies and elevates the wreath of my happiness through fragrance, form, and color to the utmost.
> —*Maria Dietrich*

cloud nine (or seven) *n* a state of great happiness (synonyms: bliss, blissfulness, seventh heaven)

> Oh, she's off on Cloud Seven—doesn't even know we exist.　　—*O. Duke*

fun *n* something that is pleasant and enjoyable and makes you feel happy

It's kind of fun to do the impossible.

—*Walt Disney*

halcyon *adj* calm, peaceful, happy

[Halcyon derives from Greek halkuon, *a mythical bird, kingfisher. This bird was fabled by the Greeks to nest at sea, about the time of the winter solstice, and, during incubation, to calm the waves.]*

Peace and policy had diffused a halcyon calmness over the land.   —*B. Disraeli*

hope *n* a feeling of desire and expectation that things will go well in the future

Hope is itself a species of happiness, and, perhaps, the chief happiness which this world affords.   —*Samuel Johnson*

living *adj* having life; being alive

Be happy while you're living, for you're a long time dead.   —*Scottish proverb*

love *n* a strong liking for something or someone; a passionate feeling of romantic desire and sexual attraction or an intense feeling of tender affection and compassion

The grand essentials of happiness are:
something to do, something to love,
something to hope for.
>   —*Allan K. Chalmers*

luscious *adj* delicious, sweet; also, of a woman,
sexually attractive; of food, juicy or very good
to eat
[Middle English lucius, alteration of licious, perhaps short for delicious]
>   Worm that . . . Eats the life out of every
>   luscious plant.   —*Robert Browning*

puppy *n* a young dog
>   Happiness is a warm puppy.
>   —*Charlie Brown*

PART 4: MISCELLANEOUS

Though the exercises in Part 4 are not based on making a list, mind map, or journal entry, you can easily transform them into a writing practice by employing one of those methods.

158) Training Yourself to Notice Details and Look Up Answers to Questions That Arise through Observation

Most people go through life not paying attention to the little things, the details, the curiosities around them. Your brain automatically "takes note" in some cases. When you go for a walk, you do not have to look down at the ground the whole way. You look ahead and your brain records certain things about the terrain that allows you to walk smoothly over it. But this is not the case for everything. For a lot of the details of life, you have to train yourself to "take note."

Pick one thing to look at closely, in the room or space where you are now. Try for something you know is there and you take for granted, something you have not studied in any way.

Look at your jeans. Have you noticed that blue jeans are sewn with orange thread? Why is that? I looked it up, and the reason Levi Strauss did this was to match the copper rivets (which are there, by the way, to double the durability of the jeans).

Look at your cat. Why does she knead her paws in the pillow? This behavior is a remnant from kittenhood, sometimes called the "milk tread" because it is done during nursing so the kitten gets more milk from the mommy. It is speculated that as adults, the behavior is continued as an expression of comfort when the animal is feeling safe and happy, so your cat may be associating the contentment she gets from being with you with happy memories of time spent with her mother.

There is so much knowledge to be gained in this world that you will never be at a loss to find material to learn about. It is important to keep your brain active throughout your entire lifetime. Your brain needs exercise just like your body does. These learning activities enrich your life. They take your mind off its wanderings into the past and future. You are in the present moment when you are learning. And what you learn can become part of your conversations with others, creating stronger and livelier interconnections.

_____

_____

_____

_____

_____

_____

_____

_____

_____

159) Finding Something to Be Happy About in a Mundane Activity/Task

Yes, there they are again—the dishes. Didn't you just do them? These are the dishes from a small casual lunch and someone's coffee cup.

Okay, not a big deal—let's just do them and get it over with. Wait. Did you do that with your:

breakfast
cup of coffee
shower
makeup
e-mail check
cleaning the cat box
vacuuming
et cetera

already today? How many of these things did you do on autopilot? Were you even there during each of those (mundane) activities or tasks—or had Elvis left the building?

You may not want to spend that much more time doing these things, but do you want to count them as lost moments and minutes, time thrown away because there was no awareness or presence at the time? You can bring your focus to what you are doing and stay in the moment—even creating a Zen moment—by breathing and slowing down and focusing on the activity instead of either zoning out or following your monkey mind wherever it takes you (past, future?). Enjoy the struggle. You can stop having that continual conversation with yourself and "just" wash the dishes. You might see a bubble form and rise. You might hear the squeak of the brush on the dish. You might feel the silky goodness of the water. See, *you are here!*

_____

_____

_____

_____

_____

160) Creating a Happiness Mantra

A mantra is a word or phrase that is repeated in meditation or prayer. The object is to choose a mantra that either brings you happiness, sends happiness to others, or focuses on a change you need to make in order to be happier. Examples are:

I am happy and aware.

May all beings have happiness.

May I be calm and quiet.

Write in your journal about your choice of mantra. Was it easy to choose? What feeling does it give you when you use it? When do you use it? Do you notice a difference in your life if you keep practicing it? Should you share your mantra?

_____

_____

_____

_____

_____

_____

_____

_____

161) Choosing a Happiness Quotation for Every Room

There are lots of quotations concerning happiness. Select a different quote for every room. First, collect them in your journal and assign the rooms. Write a note about why each is appropriate for each room. Then type up the quotes or write them on sticky notes.

Use websites like Bartleby (www.bartleby.com/quotations/), Think-Exist (http://en.thinkexist.com/), and The Quotations Page (www.quotationspage.com/search.php3),

After these quotes have been up for a week, come back and write in your journal about them. Do you still look at them? Do others in your household? Do you think they are useful or silly? Do you plan to replace them on a regular basis? Did you benefit from the exercise of finding them in the first place?

This exercise can also be done at work. Find a happiness quote and place it somewhere in your office, on your desk or at your workstation. What kind of reaction do you get from coworkers? Does it brighten up your work area?

Whether at home or at work, you will be surprised at the different reactions you get from the quotes.

---

162) Finding Something Yellow When You Are Irritated

Yellow is a happy color, and it's also a symbol of clarity, peace, inner strength, and motivation. Here is a little trick you can use: When you are feeling irritated or annoyed, look around for something yellow

(like a taxi, school bus, hat, house, ball, flower, *National Geographic,* rain slicker, mustard, car, picture, painting, book).

By focusing on the color yellow, hopefully you will be able to let go of the thing that is bothering you. When you do this, make a note of it in your journal. Did it work? Was this helpful in relieving your feelings of irritation and annoyance? What was your reaction the second you spotted the color yellow?

---

163) Create a Mindfulness Routine for Overcoming a Habit Like Overeating or Becoming Angry

Let's look at some habits you would like to change or address. First, select a couple of important ones; then, write about how you would like to change them, but also write about what you see as their root or cause. If you ignore the cause, you may be able to change the habit for a little while, but it won't be a permanent change. If your habit has an impact on other people, it is important to understand why. This exercise tries to help you deal with the habit, in the long term. You may experience stumbling blocks here. Don't be discouraged. Each day offers you the chance to do better.

Bringing mindfulness to these areas is going to help. Habits are generally mindless, done on autopilot when the root/cause triggers them. One of the best mindfulness practices is slowing down or pausing when you are about to carry out your usual reaction (like anger) or action (like overeating). Determine to increase your mindfulness from moment to moment.

_____

_____

_____

_____

_____

_____

164) Leaving Happiness Notes for Others

Caring about the happiness of others is the best thing you can do for them—and for yourself. The more you do for others, the happier you will be. One way is to allow others more freedom, space, and time. Practice listening intently to others, showing respect for others' time. Help others. This is not an exercise where you should expect something back from other people. Your reward is how your actions toward others affect you.

You can actively add happy moments to others' lives by leaving happiness notes in purses, briefcases, or on mirrors. You can send happy e-mails or postcards. Remember that all the happiness in the world comes from thinking of others. Don't be surprised if people begin to expect these notes from you, and perhaps start giving their own.

_____

_____

_____

_____

_____

_____

165) Read Something That You Want to Read, Not Something That You Feel Compelled to Read

Sure, there are things we must read—work-related documents, professional journals, maybe even a newspaper to stay up-to-date, and textbooks for the student. But the rest of one's reading should be "for fun"—whatever that is for you. Sometimes our busy lives get in the way, but if you focus on this exercise, you will find the time. Keep a journal entry open on the things that you choose to read. See if you recognize any patterns or themes in the material you choose.

With all that there is to choose from, this should be easy, but somehow we manage to complicate it by feeling we must read things on the best-seller list, or something inspirational, or something practical. However, if you feel like reading a comic book or a cookbook, or even a dictionary, you really should. Your brain has an instinct for what it wants for nourishment, just like your taste buds and stomach do for their food. Feed your brain with things it wants to read.

_____

_____

_____

_____

_____

_____

_____

_____

166) Create an "Altar" on Your Desk or by Your Bed—Not Necessarily Religious, but More Spiritual and Cheering

Altar is just one word for a collection of family photos, trinkets, and a vase of flowers. The idea is that the place where you work, or wherever you spend a lot of time, should be cheering and inspirational.

A desktop or bedside "altar" can help you create a sense of calm. To collect items for such an altar, stick to simple objects that are linked to a specific memory, belief, or goal. That might mean a special shell, stone, photograph, flower, fountain, book, plant, or even a quote or simple saying, like one from a fortune cookie.

What makes your collection an altar is your intention, which can be as simple as your desire to return to the present moment and become aware of it each time you see your special collection.

167) Seek Out a Good-News News Story Every Day, Especially to Share

Reading newspapers and news articles online can be depressing and confusing. We are reminded all the time of the bad things that happen every day. But there are many good things that happen daily, too. They just don't sell more copies of newspapers and magazines or produce higher ratings like the bad-news stories do. Each day, look for a good-news story. You might have to learn where to look; you might even have to dig a little. Eventually, you will find one (DOG AND FAMILY REUNITED AFTER FIVE YEARS).

Then, share this good news with someone. If you cannot find a good-news story, at least find a good clean joke to laugh at and share with a friend!

---

168) Wake Up and Smile; Other Times of the Day, Try to Make Yourself Happy with the Aid of Your Facial Muscles or Try a Laughter Exercise

In the morning when you wake up, aspire to keep a wide-open heart and mind. As you wake up, welcome the new day with a mindful smile. Your smile should help you focus on the fact that you have the entire day, your entire life in front of you. Approach it with an open heart and mind. Remember, when you smile, the whole world smiles with you.

Then, many times throughout the day, use a smiley face or laugh-ter to get yourself into the feelin'-good mode again. Get into the habit of this exercise. This wakes you up throughout the day. Take a few mo-ments and practice a half smile. Let go entirely. The smile you send out returns to you, and smiling relaxes hundreds of muscles, making your face more attractive. Begin this exercise right now. How does it feel?

_____

_____

_____

_____

_____

169) Open Up Your Options for Using Simple Means to Raise Your Spirits

There are a lot of little things you can do for yourself. It's part of tak-ing care of yourself, to look after your needs and supply yourself with small pleasures or little rewards. These are not selfish acts that cause negative feelings.

If you are a commuter, it might be having a book on tape in the car, or the promise of coffee and a croissant as soon as you get to the office. If you work at home, it might be some stretches and a cup of tea at 10 a.m. and 2 p.m. If you are a stay-at-home parent, it might be the twenty minutes you take for meditation after the kids go to bed or when they take a nap.

Whatever you choose to do should replenish you, add to your pleasure and fulfillment, nurture calmness or patience or general happiness. You know how it feels to deny yourself these types of things—self-righteous for a moment, but unpleasant later—especially when you realize how important it is to savor every moment of life.

---

170) Train Yourself to Look, Listen, or Feel Intensely in Order to Forget Everything Else (Even Yourself), and Develop Your Powers of Concentration

Whenever you can find time for just being, drop all doing. This is a moment of utter relaxation and concentration. Whenever you can, be interested in doing one very simple thing in the moment. Think of each moment as a one-pointed concentration. "Zen is not some kind of excitement, but concentration on usual everyday routine," said Shunryu Suzuki.

You can train yourself to have more concentration by becoming involved in flow activities. To experience *flow*, you must have clear goals to strive for. Then you must become immersed in the activity, paying attention to what is happening and learning to enjoy the immediate experience. No outside influences. When a baseball player is in the batter's box, he does not hear anything else around him. He has total concentration at that moment. Ted Williams said he concentrated so much when he was in the batter's box that he could see the red seams of the baseball as it was coming toward him. You can use the same type of concentration to help you study for a test, complete a work project, or listen to your child tell a story. You will see positive results. To achieve this requires determination and discipline, but it's well worth the effort.

_____

_____

_____

_____

_____

_____

_____

171) You Hear More and More about Karma These Days, but Do You Understand It?

The law of karma teaches you that you have a choice in each new moment regarding what response your heart and mind will bring to your situation. Simply said, good karma is created by planting positive seeds, having faith, being good, and waiting patiently.

It is all about cause and effect: good cause creates good effect. This is basic stuff, like not lying, not gossiping; purifying one's thoughts, actions, and words to be beneficial, not harmful. Write about your understanding of karma, and also about what you don't understand, or any questions you might have about karma. If you don't understand something or have a question, do some research to get an answer. The research may provide you with valuable information.

Here are a few ways to introduce good karma into your life:

Keep your food simple.

Create your ultimate to-do list, one that helps you chart
    your path.

Listen to the whole answer.

Clean your house with all-natural ingredients.

Regardless of the situation, react with class and dignity.

_____

_____

_____

_____

_____

_____

172) Good or Bad, Accept Everything as an Opportunity to Learn

Think of how long you have been here on Earth and all the opportunities you have been granted to learn. How many have you taken full advantage of? Remember, these can be good or bad opportunities. Write them in your journal.

Refused to take piano lessons when I was a child.

Lost out on a great job opportunity.

Was asked to coach a child's basketball team.

Read a book about Henry David Thoreau.

It is time now to learn, especially about the nature of the universe and your existence, and to understand that you are here for only a limited time. You need to take advantage of everything, good or bad, as an opportunity to learn—or the opportunity will be gone.

Approach new experiences as opportunities to learn rather than occasions to succeed or fail. Doing so opens you up to new possibilities and can increase your sense of happiness.

---

173) Choices of Actions and Speech, Choices about Timing, and Silence and Nonaction

Be aware that we are all interdependent with everything and everyone else. Even your smallest, least significant thought, word, or action has real consequences throughout the universe. Focus on your actions and take responsibility for them.

Commit for a period of time to pay close attention to your motivations and intentions. Keep asking yourself "Why?" about anything, from small to large actions. If you do something you do not feel good about, ask why. If you do something you are proud of, ask why. If you stay mindfully aware of the whole context of every interaction, you will also remember to be extra careful when you are vulnerable.

---

174) Meditate to Remove Distraction and Mind Clutter, Doing Nothing

Investigate your distractions and mind clutter. Be an observer. Do not try to name them or react or judge. A distraction is just a distraction. If a thought (or series of them) bombards you, acknowledge this and then let it go.

By meditating and training yourself to do nothing, you will find that your mind gets better at immersing itself in an activity. Just like an athlete or a musician improves by practicing skills, so will your ability to remove distractions and mind clutter improve by practicing the simple act of doing nothing. You will find you are less plagued by distractions, desires, and fragmentation. Your daily existence will become much more satisfying.

Remember, wildflowers grow on their own. Doing nothing is often more than enough.

_____

_____

_____

_____

_____

175) Seek Out Personal Quiet Time—Resisting the Idea That It's a Waste of Time or It's Not Working for You

We live in a very busy and noisy world. Think about how life was less busy and much quieter 100 years ago, 200 years ago, 500 years ago, 1,000 years ago, 10,000 years ago. It is only in recent times that the world has become extremely busy and very noisy. Man has probably not adapted to this yet, in an evolutionary sense. We need to experience quiet time in order to balance the busyness and loudness of life. Seek out and take advantage of quiet time.

It is common to think of time spent doing nothing as a "waste"—but it is actually just the opposite. Everyone needs to pause, slow down, stop, breathe, and do nothing. By doing so, you are developing a sense of calm awareness, patience, a protective aura, a center. This is something that will come in handy, possibly even save you, many times in the future. Extreme quiet and stillness are original naturalness. The quieter you become, the more you can hear. There is music in silence.

---

176) Discover Compartmentalization to Remove Thoughts and Park Your Problems for Mental Fitness

You can do this on a piece of paper or even in meditation—put items in "compartments," depending on certain criteria.

Things I Worry About but Can Do Nothing About
Things I Should Take Steps to Deal With
Problems I Cannot Solve without Help
Useless Thoughts
Thoughts That May Become Ideas

These are a few examples. By compartmentalizing them, you can deal with what you need to and basically "throw away" the rest.

You begin to understand and get a grip on what you need to do. Some things will be significant while others will be unimportant. You now have the tool to focus on the important issues. The inconsequential things can be discarded. You are mentally cleaning house.

You can also use this method to "park" your distracting thoughts and feelings, saying to yourself, "I will come back to this thought later" by setting aside a specific time to worry, feel sad or angry, seek solutions, etc. We only have so much time and energy to handle everything that we need to in life. When we compartmentalize our thoughts, we can focus on the significant ones first. The time and energy that you would have used to think about and dwell on unimportant thoughts can now be used to handle the important issues in your life. This technique will help you become more efficient in your ability to handle things.

_____

_____

_____

_____

_____

_____

_____

_____

_____

_____

177) Choose a Breathing Exercise That Helps Raise Your Spirits

Breathing exercises can change how you feel quite dramatically. The second you choose to mind your breath, you have decided that this present moment is worthy of your attention. You have begun to extri cate yourself from the hold of the past and the pull of the future. You are living your life as of today. That in itself is invigorating!

Perform *fire breathing* before a meditation session. Take a deep breath, filling your lungs, then exhale in quick snorts, rapidly contracting and releasing your stomach muscles. Do this for a minute or two to oxygenate the blood and raise *prana* (the life force) in your system.

Try a *dynamic meditation*. In the first ten minutes, breathe rapidly in and out through the nose, letting the breath be intense and cha-otic. Allow your body to move with this fast breath, especially moving your arms. Then for ten minutes, give your body freedom to express itself—just ·explode! Sing, scream, laugh, shout, cry, jump, shake, dance, kick, whatever. Do not hold back. For the next ten minutes, let your neck and shoulders relax while you raise your arms and shout the mantra "HOO HOO HOO" while jumping up. Make sure you land on the flat part of your feet. Then for fifteen minutes, stop. Freeze where you are. Just be. Then in the final fifteen minutes, celebrate with more dancing and singing, even to music if you wish.

Try the following Qigong exercise called "Scooping the Stream":

Stand, feet together, hands loosely by your sides, eyes fixed on a point ahead. Inhale slowly as you raise your arms above your head and in-terlace your fingers, palms facing up. Stretch your body up to its full extent, heels on the ground. Ex-hale slowly as you lower your arms to your sides. Pause and repeat. Then, bring your hands in front of your navel, palms turned up, and interlace your fingers to form a scoop. Slowly inhale while raising your arms to bring the scoop up to your lips, like you are drinking water, with your elbows as high as possible. Hold this for a count of three. Turn your palms down and lower your arms again, exhaling slowly. Repeat the whole sequence six times.

---

178) Become Consciously Aware of Your Reaction to Whatever Happens, and When You Feel a Negative Reaction, Look For the Positive

Be aware of actions, emotional states, intentions, mental and physical reactions. It is easier for us to witness negative behavior in other people than in ourselves. We have the ability to justify our own negative responses. Once we realize that even if we can justify our old, conditioned emotional reactions, it doesn't make them right—then we've taken the first step toward changing them.

Ask yourself, What should I let go of? What has to be accepted? What lesson might I learn from this? What is the hidden value or positive element of this situation?

Look for the good in everything. The trick is to see everything in both a realistic light and a positive light at the same time. When you notice a negative thought arising, observe it without judgment before replacing it with a positive thought.

179) Try for a Day to Be a Great Actor (If You Act It, You Become It)—You Become What You Act, Think, Say

Several wise writers have said, "You become what you think about all day long," or variations on this theme. Just like the old adage "You are what you eat." So, to test this theory, try for a day to be a great actor. If you act, think, or speak it—you become it. Spread your wings and soar.

So be your "ultimate self"—the person you dream of being or say you would be if all of your "if onlys" were taken care of. Ignore all circumstances and be that person for a day. Lose the persona of the person you are and change it to your "ultimate self."

How did it feel—real or fake? Was it natural or stiff? Any short-term or long-term effects? Can you do it again?

---

180) Give in Any Way You Can—Time, Help, Money, Stuff— Push Yourself to Be More Generous Than You Have Been in the Past

Practice acting on thoughts of generosity that arise in your mind. Undertake for one week to act on every single thought of generosity that arises spontaneously in your heart. Generosity even refers to how you respond to situations.

Think about the areas in your family, community, and the world in which you would like to develop more generosity. Actively look for more opportunities to give of your time, energy, money, goods, love, or service to others.

Only by being fully present and cultivating gratitude, generosity, and kindness can we find the renewable source of happiness in ourselves in each moment.

---

181) Learn to Phrase What You Say Positively and to Take Responsibility for What You Say

Remember that *how* you say something is as important as *what* you say. Before you say something, ask yourself whether your words will build or harm the relationship. It is how, when, and why you say things—not just *what* you say.

Consider each word carefully before you say anything—so your speech is "right" in both form and content. Let your words be straightforward and simple.

When you change what you say to "right" speech, you will notice that people will recognize the change. They may not be able to define what is different, but they will recognize that something has changed positively. Imagine never having to regret anything you say!

_____

_____

_____

_____

_____

_____

182) Drift

Let your mind drift for a few minutes. Watch the clouds floating by or the fish swimming in an aquarium; observe the wind in the trees or grass, a fire in the fireplace, stars in the night sky. Let go and let be. Observe the mind without judgment.

Periodically, allow yourself some time to do this exercise. When you drift in nature, you become one with it. Where are you when you drift? Allow yourself to do this exercise often. Be one with nature. Drift.

_____

_____

_____

_____

_____

183) Venting

Practice venting your feelings in a safe way, through sound—like a deep breath, a moan, chant, groan, or shout. Let it out until you need to breathe again. Like a teakettle about to boil, if you don't let the heat out, it can explode. Your body is like the teakettle. You need to vent the excess feelings and emotions so you don't explode inside.

This can be done out loud if it will not disturb or upset others. You should find another place or way to do it if people or animals are in your vicinity. Sometimes a physical release, such as sound or breath, is just what you need. Make sure you release everything when you vent. Clear out the space so new, more positive feelings and emotions can take their place.

Toning (making a steady sound with varying tones), chanting, and other self-generated sounds have transforming effects on the mind and emotions. You can augment sounds with mental images of stress being washed or blown away.

_____

_____

_____

_____

_____

_____

184) Stretch

Stretch for a minute or two at a time, as often as you can remember to do so throughout your workday, evening leisure time, etc.

Envision a large, happy lion, stretching and roaring. Raise your arms and spread them wide, with palms forward. Give praise to the earth and sky. Fill your insides with the emptiness around you. Stretch restores flexibility, helps you to relax, and realigns your body. Feel the physical change in your body when you stretch. The blood will flow through your body more efficiently, thus positively affecting your mind.

Contemplate emptiness stretching away in every direction. Meditate on this emptiness and be free.

_____

_____

_____

_____

_____

185) Comfort and Reassurance

Practice asking for comfort and reassurance, but also give support to others and yourself. It is true that you have to take care of yourself before you can help others—like putting on your oxygen mask first on an airplane and then assisting other passengers.

You can be the light that provides solace in the darkness. Holding people or offering other physical closeness is one way. You can supply or maintain structure in daily life. You can offer to talk and listen. You can provide relaxing, therapeutic experiences. Just remember to take some time to deal with your own feelings and needs, so you can provide comfort and reassurance to others. When you experience what it is like to comfort and reassure yourself, you will have the know-how and confidence to do the same for others.

_____

_____

_____

_____

_____

186) Inner Dialogues

Practice changing your inner dialogues— or stopping them altogether. Stop from time to time during the day and pay attention to your inner dialogue. You are NOT your thoughts, and you need to train yourself NOT to believe the messages they give.

When you have a constant dialogue with yourself, become aware and say to yourself, "Stop talking."

When you stop, note what the voices in your head were jabbering about. What is the theme or themes? What is the emotional tone? Watch for when the talking starts again, like a tennis player watches for the ball. Remember, you are not your thoughts, and you do not have to believe the messages they impart.

---

187) Inspire with Love

Inspire your partner with love and practice bringing out the best in him or her (or a child for a parent, or a friend for a friend). Watch for acts of beauty in yourself and others and use them for inspiration. Act upon inspirational words you read.

Love the people in your life by acting in harmonious ways, by bringing awareness to your behavior, by acting with integrity. Love them as you would like to be loved. It is a simple rule to follow, with powerful results. Can you love without interfering? Can you love without imposing your will through manipulation or aggressive emotions and actions? Open up and love—today. You will see the inspiration and love grow mutually.

188) Volunteer

Volunteer to assist in a community project or organization that really connects with your values. Volunteering is a wonderful way to give back to the world for all you are appreciative for. You can volunteer:

at a children's school
as a docent
by running errands for the sick or elderly
by leading a youth group
at a recreation program
on a hotline
at a zoo
by training a Seeing Eye dog
with Meals on Wheels
as a Big Brother or Sister
as a reading tutor
for a beach cleanup
for Head Start
at a nursing home
for a fire department
to cuddle premature infants
as a tutor in public schools
at an animal shelter
at a people shelter
at a hospice
for the children's ward of a
    hospital
for the Special
    Olympics
other good causes

_____

189) Creative Realizations Come When the Brain Is Relaxed, Solitary, Peaceful—So Schedule Daydreaming into Your Days

We have introduced meditation in this book, which is one highly recommended method of letting your brain go a little. Daydreaming is another way to pay close attention while you relax and find peace. Daydreaming is also a great way to solve problems. Setting aside ten minutes a day to daydream is a meditation in itself. Staring at an outdoor scene is really not very different from closing your eyes or gazing at a candle. If your mind starts wandering, just come back to the breath and the scene. You're not stopping daydreaming, just using this method to observe daydreaming. See what happens when you embrace the art of daydreaming.

Try to see and feel your surroundings, or close your eyes and relax your breathing. Let this shift your brain into its nerve-connective symphony.

_____

190) Try Having a Good Conversation

Try having a good conversation that is like a jam session, starting with conventional elements and then introducing spontaneous variations that create an exciting new composition. It is important to eliminate any negative tone, to be really honest during the exchange, and to spend a lot of time listening. You should be asking questions more often than telling your own stories or expressing your personal opinions. Good conversation consists of talking about everything, and nothing at all.

Relish the pauses and also trust the flow within the conversation. Make a conscious effort to relax your breathing during the conversation and focus on listening to the other person, and above all, to maintain control over what you are saying.

---

191) Create Something You Can Tend To

Create something you can tend to and nurture: flowers, herbs, plants, an entire garden, get a pet. The rewards are numerous.

You are often tending to the little rips, tears, and loose buttons of life. But how about tending something where you are actually nurturing growth?

If you are not already the proud owner of some plants or a garden, now is the time to get started. The same goes for having a pet, a living creature that you will care for and nurture and play with. Tend to these meditatively. Be a gardener of life.

_____

_____

_____

_____

_____

192) Look for Self-Contained Activities

Look for self-contained activities, ones that are done not with the expectation of some future benefit, but simply because the doing itself is the reward. This is an important skill to develop and can be applied to anything you undertake. It teaches you to be in the moment and not rely on a future thank-you or acknowledgment. You often get distracted by your expectations regarding the results of an activity. This exercise is a practice in divesting yourself of all expectations.

reading three pages of the dictionary each day.
waxing the car
alphabetizing the spice rack
anonymously donating used books for the upcoming library sale
brushing the cat's fur

So, select an activity just for your own learning or pleasure. Do not expect anything. Have an open mind and step humbly through the doorway. Carry out the activity and be content with whatever comes.

_____

_____

_____

_____

_____

_____

193) Happy Activities

Focus on doing happy activities that require few or no material resources but which demand a high investment of psychological energy.

Perceiving, remembering, thinking, feeling, wishing, willing, attending, and striving are all psychological activities. Make a list here of what you could engage in as happy activities involving one or more of these energies.

do a relaxation exercise

go for a walk

read an interesting article

do some creative writing

meditate for twenty minutes

_____

_____

_____

_____

_____

_____

_____

_____

194) Add Dance

Add dance to your life in a way that makes sense for you and brings you happiness. Take up an expressive form of dance or movement. You can do this when no one is around if you feel self-conscious. Dance when the spirit moves you. Dance a little bit every day.

Viennese waltz

Charleston

tap dance

cha-cha

frug

Dance can also be total meditation. You can dance with your
eyes closed and let your unconscious take over. Do not "control" your movements. Disappear in the dance. Dance like a tree. "Speak" in movement and flow. Dance as if you are expressing your gratitude for living. In general, let life be more of a dance and less of a battle.

195) Yoga

Yoga produces tremendous physical and mental flow. If you have never tried it, try it. If you do it, do more. Yoga improves health, increases flexibility, heals aches and pains, keeps sickness at bay, and increases energy. Sounds like happiness!

There is so much variety in yoga, and you can do it almost anywhere, like in a space on the bedroom floor, in a hotel room, outside on a porch. You do not need much, and it won't take long to find the type of yoga you like best. Here is a simple sun salutation:

> mountain pose with prayer hands
> (*namaste*)
> mountain pose arms overhead
> standing forward bend
> downward dog
> plank
> cobra
> downward dog
> standing forward bend
> mountain pose arms overhead to *namaste*

Yoga is an active meditation and addresses the biological component of happiness as well. Yoga changes your consciousness and your brain chemistry in a positive way.

_____

_____

_____

_____

_____

_____

_____

_____

196) Art and Conscious Seeing

Visual skills can provide constant access to enjoyable experiences. Add art and *conscious seeing* to your life in ways that feel good to you. *Conscious seeing* is a process of living in a more aware state through the eyes.

While you may appreciate the beauty around you, you may not feel confident about doing art on your own. It is hard to teach yourself to let go of judgment and doubt, but art really is therapeutic, and we all have some sort of creative drive inside of us. Often, the type of art you are drawn to is the type of art you should try to create.

_____

_____

_____

_____

_____

_____

_____

_____

197) Food

Take the time to really see, taste, chew, and experience food—one of the basic pleasures built into your nervous system. Doing this will change your whole relationship with food, for the better.

The first thing to do is see the food and be aware of that seeing. Then there is your intention to eat the food, a mental process. The mental intention becomes the cause of your arm moving. Then the intention to lift your arm, and the lifting. Opening the mouth. Putting in the food. Closing the mouth. The intention to lower your arm, then the movement itself. Feeling the food in your mouth and its texture. Chewing and experiencing the movement. As the chewing begins, there will be taste sensations. Being mindful of the taste. Swallowing.

Being mindful of the sequence of processes, getting free of the concepts, seeing the continuity, the interrelationships—all of this will heighten your enjoyment of food.

_____

_____

_____

_____

_____

_____

_____

198) Pastime

Choose an inexpensive and portable pastime that is simple and illuminating—like crossword puzzles, word games, Sudoku, spelling quizzes, vocabulary tests, etc. Though there are times when doing nothing—simply waiting, breathing, or meditating—are perfect for you, portable pastimes are for other times when you want to feed the brain.

Define:

advantage *n*

beautify *v*

cloud nine (or seven) *n*

fun *n*

halcyon *adj*

hope *n*

living *adj*

love *n*

luscious *adj*

puppy *n*

See #157 for author's answers.

These types of activities are creative and stretch the brain's "muscles." Even carrying a notebook or journal for writing while on the go is a perfect portable pastime. These offer a great break amid routine activity in a nontrivial way.

_____

_____

_____

_____

_____

_____

_____

_____

199) Science

Become an amateur scientist in an area that truly intrigues you, from meteorology to astronomy. There are many areas of study you can choose from. The mental framework that makes science enjoyable is accessible to everyone: curiosity, careful observation, disciplined recording of events, etc.

- Look up in the sky and see all the stars. Think back to a time before the telescope was invented and imagine what people thought of the nighttime sky.
- Keep a weather chart, observing daily weather patterns.
- Sow some seeds in a pot or small garden and discover how to cultivate them.

There's no reason why you cannot bring the pleasure and excitement of designing a "science fair project" into your life again. You might even make an original discovery!

_____

_____

_____

_____

_____

_____

_____

200) Hobbies and Interests

Look for hobbies and personal interests that demand skill and make leisure what it is supposed to be: re-creation. The flow experience that results from the use of skills leads to growth.

Ask yourself what makes a hobby rewarding for you. Do you end up with a physical manifestation, something you can use or display? Do you use your creative side or a part of you that is not involved in your job or career? Your hobbies and interests may be a real opportunity for flow—for exploring the potential of the self. The world is absolutely full of interesting things to do.

---

201) Getting Stuck

If you ever get stuck on something, get up and do something else. You get your best ideas and solutions when you rest.

Check in with yourself. Do you feel "not quite right" about what you are engaged in? Set it aside and wait for something to be revealed—a word, image, or feeling. When something comes to you, ask "Is this right?"

Another approach when you feel stuck is to find an object of love. Love is flow, and you will suddenly feel your energy flowing again.

Whenever you feel stuck, frustrated, or limited, pick up and change what your mind is dwelling on. Try to focus on the breath and let go. Accept and be aware that we all have moments of getting stuck. Let go and settle into the moment.

_____

_____

_____

_____

_____

_____

202) Attention

Pay attention to what is happening in this moment. Concentration leads to involvement, wholeheartedly taking part without self-consciousness. Being in control of the mind means anything that happens can literally be a source of joy.

Through mindful attention and nonattachment, you can make your daily life sacred by practicing restraint, morality, and sincere virtue. Doing anything with mindful awareness can be an effective meditation.

_____

_____

_____

_____

_____

_____

_____

203) Jell-O

To think outside the box, make a bowl of yellow Jell-O, and then tell it your troubles. It is like a Zen koan: Your brain cannot think in an ordinary way when you are talking to Jell-O. Your brain gets unstuck from its old ways of thinking and communicating. Here are some of the many Jell-O possibilities:

Jell-O jigglers
layered Jell-O parfait
congealed salad
the smooth surface of Jell-O
Jell-O pudding
Jell-O shimmying
blocks of Jell-O
layered Jell-O
reaching blindfolded
    into a bowl of
    Jell-O
lettuce under Jell-O
squishing Jell-O in your
    teeth

---

204) Silence

Learn to tolerate silence. Do not let it intimidate you. Embrace it. Listen instead. Relax in the quiet that contains the mind. In a world full of noise, silence can be a scary thing. But when you embrace silence, it becomes a friend. It becomes an important part of your life because it enables you to focus on the present.

> We can make our minds so like still water that beings gather about us to see their own images and so live for a moment with a clearer, perhaps even fiercer life because of our silence.
>
> —William Butler Yeats

---

205) Decompression

Take some decompression time—five to ten minutes, or a half-hour, alone—and create a ritual that works for you. It can be breathing, meditating, walking, stretching, and so on.

Look away from what you are doing. Breathing out, let your mind decompress, simply *be*, relaxing in the experience for the time.

_____

_____

_____

_____

_____

_____

206) Water

As humans, 99 percent of the time, our bodies feel air around us. Water offers us an invigorating alternative to air. Soak in a tub of hot water or float in a heated pool. See the water flowing, running deep. Feel the water and notice how different it is from air. Rid yourself of impurities and feel the

energy of the water. Let the water take you back to the time before your birth and a deep-seated sense of renewal. Let the water carry away discomfort and distress, leaving you feeling refreshed and invigorated. Feel the water. Be mindful. Rest in the water. Let tension drain away. Rest, relax, breathe slowly. Melt into the water.

Or meditate on the water in an aquarium. Water flows, never fights, around the objects it meets. Let the water carry you to happiness.

_____

_____

_____

_____

_____

_____

_____